AF552904

RENEWABLE RESOURCES AND ENVIRONMENT

RENEWABLE RESOURCES AND ENVIRONMENT

Chief Editor

Dr. Baby Tabassum
Assistant Professor
Department of Zoology
Govt. Raza P.G. College, Rampur (U.P.)
President of Society
(Scientific Awareness among Rural Children)

Associate Editors

Dr. Priya Bajaj
Assistant Professor
Department of Zoology
Govt. Raza P.G. College
Rampur (U.P.)
(India)

Dr. Riyaz Z. Sayyed
Head of the Dept.
Dept. of Microbiology
PSGV P Mandal's Science College
Shahada - 425 409
(MS) (India)

DISCOVERY PUBLISHING HOUSE PVT. LTD.
NEW DELHI-110 002

Published by:
Namit Wasan

DISCOVERY PUBLISHING HOUSE PVT. LTD.
4383/4B, Ansari Road, Darya Ganj
New Delhi-110 002 (India)
Phone : +91-11-23279245, 43596064-65
Fax : +91-11-23253475
E-mail : discoverypublishinghouse@gmail.com
namitwasan9@gmail.com
sales@discoverypublishinggroup.com
web : www.discoverypublishinggroup.com

***First Edition:* 2018**

ISBN: 978-93-5056-893-4

Renewable Resources and Environment

Printed at:
Infinity Imaging Systems
Delhi

Preface

As we know renewable resources are those generated from natural sources that do not have a finite and, or those that can be recycled. As the human population increases our rate of consumption of these resources also increases. Even though renewable sources are low in price and easily available, the need to explore alternative feedstock's as well as remedies of various problems remains highly important.

The chapters of this book dealing with natural products as remedial point of view. We have given a systematic number of reading references at the end of each chapter to enable reader to extend their Knowledge and also to make up for further reading material. It is impossible to express my indebtness to authors of the chapters from which I have gained so much information and I can only hope that some measure of my gratitude is expressed by the references; I have given to their work.

I sincerely acknowledge my principal Dr. Saeeda Begum Rizwi who has given me a free hand to work and motivational support as well as affection during this entire task. Acknowledgements are due to my colligues for their suggestions and contribution. The editors are grateful to their family memembers for their whole hearted support and continuous co-operation.

Special thanks due to the publisher Mr. Tilak Wasan "Discovery Publishing House Pvt. Ltd." Who give us proper and continuous support and encourage us to share our Knowledge and wisdom not only this book but many more.

We hope this book wills provide a platform to multidisciplinary forum to explore and share their knowledge about renewable resources.

—Editors

Contents

Pages: 1-10

Renewable Resources and Environment
Edited by: Dr. Baby Tabassum
ISBN: 978-93-5056-893-4
Edition: 2018
Published by: Discovery Publishing House Pvt. Ltd., New Delhi (India)

Isolation and Identification of Various Fungal Strains as Primary Colonizers from Wheat Crop Residue at Varying Phosphorus Concentrations

Shahnaaz Khatoon[†*] S.C.Jain[†] and M.U. Charaya[‡]

ABSTRACT

A total of ten strains of fungal primary colonizers were isolated from wheat straw by using Czapek's Dox Agar medium. Out of these, only two fungi belonged to ascomycota and remaining eight belonged to deuteromycota. The media with varying phosphorus concentrations were used for the isolation of fungi from wheat straw sample through serial dilution plate method. Identification and characterization of primary colonizers were made with the help of authentic manuals of soil fungi. *Alternaria alternata, Alternaria citri, Aspergillus flavus, Aspergillus fumigatus, Aspergillus niger, A. sydowi, Aspergillus wentii, Aspergillus ustus, Cladosporium herbarum, Fusarium moniliforme* were the most frequently isolated genera at low phosphorus concentration. Therefore, these fungal species seems to be potential candidates as initial primary bioinoculants for hastening the decomposition of wheat straw.

Keywords: Wheat straw, primary colonizers, Phosphorus, ascomycota, deuteromycota, decomposition.

† Department of Botany, D.N. (P.G.) College Meerut - 200 005 (Uttar Pradesh)

‡ Department of Botany, Chaudhary Charan Singh University Meerut - 200 005 (Uttar Pradesh)

* Corresponding author' *email:* Shahnaazkhatoon@gmail.com

INTRODUCTION

Wheat is grown basically for the grains. But the utility of the remaining parts of the wheat plant cannot be ignored. A lot of wheat straw is produced in wheat-growing belts in the world. A significant proportion of wheat straw has been in use as feed for ruminants because of its abundance and low cost (Viola *et al.*, 2008; Bals *et al.*, 2010). However, it is also used for the production of pulp and paper (Zhao *et al.*, 2004), strawboards (Deswarte *et al.*, 2007), textiles and composites (Avella *et al.*, 1995; Reddy and Yang, 2007), plastics (Avella *et al.*, 1995) and for the removal of metals in wastewater industry (Kumar *et al.*, 2000; Doan *et al.*, 2008).

Incidentally, a major portion of straw is burnt in the field itself (Gupta *et al.*, 2004). This results, on one hand, in a waste of organic sources in soil affecting C:P ratio and biota; and on other hand, leads to global warming and environmental problems (Badrinath *et al.*, 2006). Keeping in mind the harmful effects of burning straw in the field as well as the convenience of farmer, economical, environment–friendly and low labour strategies should be adopted for effective utilization of the straw.

Primary colonizers are the microorganisms which play an important role in the initiation of decomposition. These organisms span parasitic as well as saprophytic phases, possess cellulolytic and pectolytic activity at low nitrogen level, and are able to grow at faster rate on a comparatively drier resource (Charaya and Mehrotra, 2005), Charaya (2006), Chauhan (2006) and Rani (2008) also found that majority of the primary colonizers of plant litter possessed weak parasitic tendency.

Organic matter plays a unique role in the soil fertility. It acts as a sink as well as a source for nutrient. It prevents environmental pollution and the loss of nutrients. Above all, it helps in maintaining nutrients balance in the soil which is the basic attribute for sustainability (Raman, 2005). In a natural ecosystem, entire biomass of the plants is returned to the soil after the death of the plants through the process of decomposition. However, in agro-ecosystems, a significant proportion of the biomass is removed from the soil. Hence, intensive cultivation of crop requires massive application of synthetic fertilizers to compensate for the loss of nutrients from the soil as a result of their removal by the agricultural crops.

However, the prohibitive cost of chemical fertilizers as also numerous environmental problems associated with their production and use have prompted the scientists to look for better alternatives. It is being gradually realized that organic wastes and biological sources of nutrients are better alternatives and these may serve as substitutes for inorganic fertilizers to a considerable extent, if not absolutely (Shukla and Mathur, 2000). Wheat straw provides one such alternative. The application of biodegraded products of straw into soil has enormous potential to recycle nutrients and maintain soil fertility (Gaind *et al.*, 2006).

In soil, the pool of soluble phosphate in solution is quite small. Much of the phosphate is adsorbed onto surfaces and there can be a great deal of phosphate in insoluble form as salts of calcium, aluminium and iron. There can be a significant fraction of phosphorus in organic compounds. The total P content of soil occurring in different agro-ecological regions of India varies widely from less than 200 ppm to over 2000 ppm. According to Tomar (1997), the total P content in soils of India varies from as low as 49 to as high as 3,580 ppm.

The microbial conversion of difficult inaccessible inorganic phosphates to accessible form in the soil plays an important role in the phosphorus feeding of plants (Babenko *et al.,* 1984). Paul and Sundara Rao (1971) isolated twelve phosphate-solubilising organisms from the rhizosphere of four cultivated legumes growing in four soil regions of India. Stotzky and Norman (1961) and Zayed *et al.* (1971) had observed that the addition of phosphorus led to an increase in the rate of decomposition.

Phosphorus status of soil and of the decomposing reported to enhance the rate of decomposition (Chekalov, 1955; Hadas *et al.*, 1998) especially in the light of the fact that soils in India are perpetually deficient in P while acute deficiencies of P are recorded in some pockets (Sharda and Mehta, 2004).

While proposing to utilize straw for direct ploughing or composting or for various other purposes involving the process of decomposition, two alternatives are available to us as far as coping with phosphorus deficiencies is concerned:

(a) to treat the straw beforehand with some phosphatic fertilizers so as to bring up their phosphorus level;

(b) to inoculate those microorganisms which have the potential to decompose the straw at low phosphorus levels.

MATERIAL AND METHOD

Freshly harvested wheat straw was collected from agricultural fields situated at village Khardoni, Meerut. The samples were collected aseptically in fresh polythene bags and brought to the laboratory for further studies. Serial dilution plate method (Waksman, 1927) was used to isolate the fungi from litter sample; 1 g of the sample was placed in 250 ml of sterile water and stirred for fifteen minutes using a magnetic stirrer to get the stock solution. 10 ml of this solution were immediately transferred to a conical flask containing 90 ml of sterile distilled water to get a suspension of 1:10 dilution. This suspension was used for the preparation of further serial dilutions (1:100, 1:1000). From the suspension of each dilution (1:10, 1:100, 1:1,000), 1 ml aliquots were transferred to each of a set of three Petri dishes followed by the addition of approximately 20 ml of cooled (45° C) and sterilized culture medium. Czapek's Dox Agar medium (Raper and Thorn, 1949) with 30 ppm of rose bengal and 30 mg of streptomycin was used for this purpose. This medium served as control and is designated as P. The media with different phosphorus concentrations were prepared (Normal, Half, One-third, One-fourth) and were designated P, P/2, P/3, P/4 respectively. The Petri dishes were observed from the third day itself when fast-growing fungi started appearing in the Petri dishes. The slow-growing fungi were transferred onto other Petri dishes just after their appearance to prevent them from being overrun by the fast growing fungi. A complete record of the fungal species and their numbers (CFUs: Colony forming units) in the Petri dishes was maintained. The identification of the fungal species was done on the basis of their morphology and cultural characteristics following Gilman (1957), Barnett and Hunter (1972), Subramanian (1971), Ellis (1971, 1976), Domsch and Gams (1972), Domsch *et al.* (1980), Nagmani *et al.* (2008).

RESULTS AND DISCUSSION

A total of ten strains of fungal primary colonizers were isolated from the wheat straw through serial diluton plate method using media containing different levels of phosphorus. Ten fungal strains were isolated as: *Aspergillus flavus, A. fumigatus, A. niger, A. sydowi, A. ustus, A. wenti, Alternaria alternata, Alternaria citri, Cladosporium herbarum* and *Fusarium moniliforme* Out of these, only 2 belonged to Ascomycota and remaining 8 strains belonged to Deuteromycota.

The dominance of Deuteromycota observed in the present study is in full agreement with the earlier reports (Hudson, 1968; Dickinson and Pugh, 1974; Hayes and Lim, 1979; Charaya, 2006; Tiwari and Charaya, 2006; Sen and Charaya, 2010). Among the Deuteromycota, the Hyphomycetes constituted the major component. 6 species belonging to Moniliaceae and 4 species belonging to Dematiaceae were obtained. Among the Moniliaceae, 6 species belonged to the genus *Aspergillus* while *Penicillium* growth was nil. It is widely believed that Aspergilli are more common in warmer regions of the world while the Penicillia are more abundant in the colder regions. The result of the present study as also those carried out by a number of workers (Waksman, 1917; Jenson, 1931; Singh and Charaya, 1975; Sen *et al.*, 2009) support the aforementioned generalization.

CONCLUSION

From the present investigation it is concluded that a total of ten fungal strains were isolated from wheat straw. Out of these, only two belonged to ascomycota and remaining eight belonged to deuteromycota were successfully identified after staining with lactophenol cotton blue based on their morphological characters and microscopic analysis.

Table 1.1

A comparison of the Total Isolate (TI), Frequency (F) and Frequency Class (FC) of fungal species isolated using media of different nitrogen levels (P, P/2, P/3, P/4) from wheat straw

Fungal Species	P			P/2			P/3			P/4		
	TI	F	FC	TI	F	FC	TI	F	FC	TI	F	FC
Alternaria alternata	1	11.11	I	–	–	–	1	11.11	I	–	–	–
A. citri	2	11.11	I	–	–	–	2	22.22	II	1	11.11	I
Aspergillus flavus	3	22.22	II	6	44.44	III	2	22.22	II	1	11.11	I
A. fumigatus	29	55.55	III	2	22.22	II	4	33.33	II	5	44.44	III
A. niger	7	66.66	IV	11	55.55	III	1	77.77	IV	5	44.44	III
A. sydowi	2	22.22	II	–	–	–	–	–	–	1	11.11	I
A. wentii	1	11.11	I	10	33.33	II	3	11.11	I	–	–	–
A. ustus	–	–	–	4	11.11	I	–	–	–	1	11.11	I
Cladosporium herbarum	2	11.11	I	6	11.11	I	7	33.33	II	–	–	–
Fusarium moniliforme	5	44.44	III	5	22.22	II	6	55.55	III	–	–	–
Total Isolates	**52**			**44**			**36**			**14**		
Total Species	**9**			**7**			**8**			**6**		

Most of concurrently which means these fungi have the capacity to decompose wheat straw at low phosphorus concentration. Therefore, these fungi have a potential to degrade wheat straw which will be tested in further study for degradation of commonly used straws.

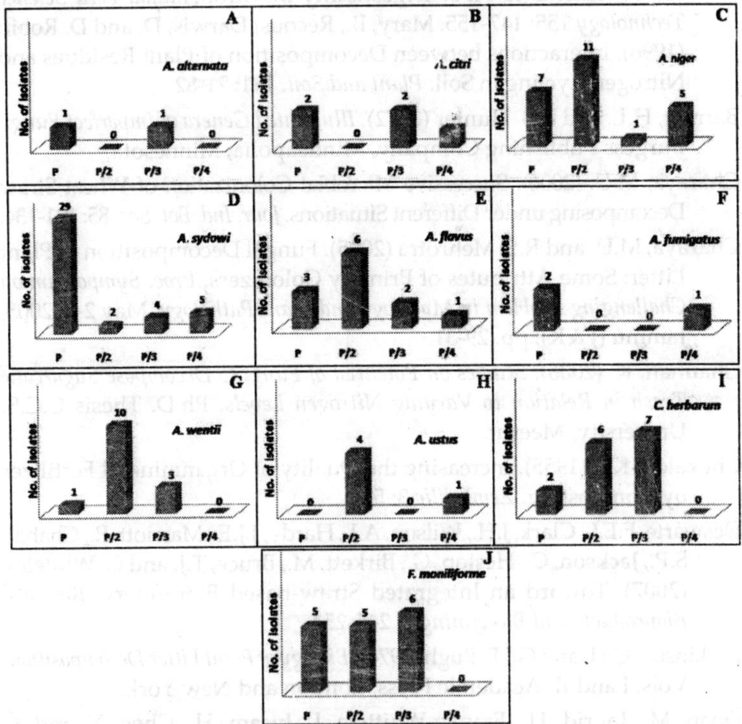

Fig. 1.1: Number of isolates of different fungal strains isolated from wheat straw using media with different phosphorous concentrations

REFERENCES

Avella, M., Bozzi, C., dell'Erba, R., Focher, B., Marzetti, A. and E. Martuscelli (1995). Steam-exploded Wheat Straw Fibers as Reinforcing Material for Polypropylene-based Composites. *Die Angew and teakro molekulare Chemie.* 233: 149-166.

Babenko, Y.S., Tyrigina, G.I., Grygoryer, L.M. and T.I. Borisova (1984). Biological Activity Physilogiobiochemical Properties of Bacteria Dissolving Phosphates. *Mikrobiologia* 53: 533-539.

Badrinath, K.V.S., Kiranchand, T.R. and Krishna Prasad (2006). Agriculture Crop Burning in the Indo-Gangetic Plains — A Study using IRS-P6AWiFS Satellite Data. *Curr. Sci.* 91: 85-89.

Bals, B., Murnen, H., Allen, M. and B. Dale (2010). Ammonia Fiber Expansion (AFEX) Treatment of Eleven Different Forages: Improvements to Fiber Digestibility in vitro. *Animal Feed Science Technology* 155: 147-155. Mary, B., Recous, Darwis, D. and D. Robin (1996). Interactions between Decomposition of Plant Residues and Nitrogen Cycling in Soil. *Plant and Soil*. 181: 71-82.

Barnett, H.L. and B.B. Hunter (1972). *Illustrated Genera of Imperfect Fungi*. Burgess Publishing Company, Minneapolia, Minnesota.

Charaya, M.U. (2006). Successive Microbial Colonization of Wheat Straw Decomposing under Different Situations. *Jour. Ind. Bot. Soc.* 85: 121-134.

Charaya, M.U. and R.S. Mehrotra (2005). Fungal Decomposition of Plant Litter: Some Attributes of Primary Colonizers. *Proc. Symposium on Challenging Problem in Mycology and Plant Pathology*. May 2-3, 2005, Jammu (J &K); pp. 29-31.

Chauhan, K. (2006). *Studies on Potential of Fungi to Decompose Sugarcane Trash in Relation to Varying Nitrogen Levels*. Ph.D. Thesis C.C.S. University, Meerut.

Chekalov, K.I. (1955). Increasing the Quality of Organmineral Fertilizer by Composting. *Zemledilic* 3: 56.

Deswarte, F.E.I., Clark, J.H., Wilson, A.J., Hardy, J.J.E., Marriott, R., Chahal, S.P., Jackson, C., Heslop, G., Birkett, M., Bruce, T.J. and G. Whiteley (2007). Toward an Integrated Straw-based Biorefinery. *Biofuels, Bioproducts and Biorefining* 1: 245-254.

Dickinson, C.H. and G.J.F. Pugh (1974). *Biology of Plant Litter Decomposition*. Vols. I and II. Academic Press, London and New York.

Doan, M., Ingrid, H., Franke-Whittele, I., Insam, H., Chen, Y. and Y. Hadar (2008). Molecular Analysis of Bacterial Community Succession during Prolonged Compost Curing. *FEMS Microbiology Ecology* 65: 133-144.

Domsch, K.H. and W. Gams (1972). *Fungi in Agricultural Soils*. Longman, London.

Domsch, K.H., Gams, W. and T. Anderson (1980). *Compendium of Soil Fungi*. Vol. I & II. Academic Press, London, New York, Sydney.

Ellis, M.B. (1971). Dematiaceous Hyphomycetes. Commonwealth Mycological Institute, Kew, Surrey, England.

Ellis, M.B. (1976). More Dematiaceous Hyphomycetes. Commonwealth Mycological Institute, Kew, Surrey, England.

Raper, K.B. and Thom (1949). A Manual of Penicillia. Williams Wilkins Co., Baltimore, Md.

Reddy N. and Y. Yang (2007). Preparation and Characterization of Long Natural Cellulose Fibers from Wheat Straw. *J. Agric. Food Chem.* 55: 8570-8575.

Sen, S. and M.U. Charaya (2010). Copper-tolerant Microfungi for Bioremediation. *Prog. Agric.* 10: 66-71.

Sen, S., Charaya, M.U. and P.B. Singh (2009). Screening of Soil for Lead Toletrant Fungi. *Indian J. Plant Genet. Resour.* 22: 191-194.

Sharda, V.N. and M. Mehta (2004). Opportunities in Microbial Diversity and Role of Biological Resources Centers. Conference on Isolation Preservation and Conservation of Agriculturally Important Microorganisms and use of Potential Molecular Tools of their Identification. NBAIM, IARI, New Delhi, pp. 31-34.

Shukla, L. and R.S. Mathur (2000). Effect of Biodegradation Sugarcane Trash on yield of Nutrient uptake by Wheat Crop. *Journal of the Indian Society of Soil Science*, 48: 520-522.

Singh, P.N. and M.U. Charaya (1975). Soil Fungi of Sugarcane Field at Meerut. Distribution of Soil Mycoflora. *Geobios.* 2: 40-43.

Stotzky, G. and A.G. Norman (1961). Factors Limiting Microbial Activities in Soil. II. The Effect of Sulphur. *Arch. Mikrobiol.* 40: 370-382.

Subramanian, C.V. (1971). *Hyphomycetes.* Indian Council of Agricultural Research, New Delhi.

Tiwari, A. (2010). *Studies on the Mitigation of Metal Pollution through Boisorption by Soil Fungi.* Ph.D. Thesis, Department of Botany, C.C.S. University, Meerut.

Tomar, K.P. (1997). *J.Indian Soc. Soil Sci.* 45: 256-261.

Viola, E., Zimbardi, F., Cardinale, M., Cardinale, G., Braccio, G. and E. Gambacorta (2008). Processing Cereal Straws by Steam Explosion in a Pilot Plant to Enhance Digestability in Ruminants. *Biores. Technol.* 99: 681-689.

Waksman, S.A. and F.G. Tenney (1927). The Composition of Natural Organic Materials and their Decomposition in the Soil. I methods of Quantitative Analysis of Plant Materials. *Soil Sci.* 24: 275-283.

Zayed, M.N., Taha, S.M. and M.A. Azazy (1971). Biological and Chemical Studies on Rice Straw Compost. V. Effect of Phosphprus. *Zentra, Apl. Bakterial. Pasteriked. Abt.* 2: 678-686.

Zhao J., Li X., Qu Y. and P. Gao (2004). Alkaline Peroxide Mechanical Pulping of Wheat Straw with Enzyme Treatment. *Appl. Biochem. Biotechnol.* 112: 12-23. Raper, K.B. and Thom (1949). A Manual of Penicillia. Williams Wilkins Co., Baltimore, Md.

Gaind, S., Pandey, A.K. and Lata (2005). Biodegradation Study of Crop Residues as Affected by Exogenous Inorganic Nitrogen and Fungal Inoculants. *J. Basic Microbiol.* 45: 301-311.

Galloway (1935), Singh and Charaya (1975), Dube *et al.* (1980), Singh (2004), Charaya (2006) and Tiwari (2010).

Galloway, L.D. (1935). Indian Soil Fungi. *Ind. J. Agric. Sci.* 6: 578-585.

Gilman, J.C. (1957). *A Manual of Soil Fungi.* Iowa State University Press, USA.

Gupta, P.K., Sahai, S., Singh, N., Dixit, C.K., Singh, D.P., Sharma, C., Tiwari, M.K., Gupta, R.K. and S.C. Garg (2004). Residue Burning in Rice Wheat Cropping System: Causes and Implications. *Curr Sci.* 87: 13-15.

Hadas, A., Parkin, T.B. and P.D. Stahl (1998). Reduced CO_2 Release from Decomposing Wheat Straw under Nitrogen Limiting Conditions: Simulation of Carbon Turnover. *European J. Soil Sci.* 49: 487-494.

Hayes, W.A. and W.G. Lim (1979). Wheat and Rice Straw Composts and Mushroom Production. In *"Straw Decay and Effect of its Diposal and Utilization"* (Ed. Gronbard, E.); John Willey and Sons, Chichester, New York, Brisbane, Toronto pp. 83-93.

Hudson, H.J. (1968). The Ecology of Fungi on Plant Remains above the Soil. *New Phytol.* 67: 837-874.

Jensen, H.L. (1931). The Fungus Flora of the Soil. *Soil Sci.* 31: 123-158.

Kumar, A., Rao, N.N. and S.N. Kaul (2000). Alkali-treated Straw and Insoluble Straw Xanthate as Low Costadsorbents for Heavy Metal Removal Preparation, Characterization and Application. *Biores. Tech.* 71: 133-142.

Nagamani, A., Kunwar, K.I.O. and C. Manoharachary (2006). *Handbook of Soil Fungi.* I.K. International Pvt. Ltd. New Delhi.

Park, D. (1976). Carbon and Nitrogen Levels as Factors Influencing Fungal Decomposers. In: *The Role of Terrestrial and Aquatic Organismsin Decomposition Process* (Eds. Anderson, J.M. and A. Macfadyen). Blackwell Scientific Publications. Oxford, London Edinburgh, Melbourne pp. 41-59.

Paul, N.B. and W.V.B. Sundara Rao (1971). Phosphate-dissolving Bacteria in the Rhizosphere of some Cultivated Legumes. *Plant and Soil* 35: 127-143.

Raman, K.V. (2005). Sustaining Soil Fertility. *The Hindu Survey of Indian Agriculture.* pp. 165-167.

Rani, P. (2008). *Studies on the Fungal Decomposition of Sugarcane Trash.* Ph.D. Thesis C.C.S. University, Meerut.

Pages: 11-18

Renewable Resources and Environment
Edited by: Dr. Baby Tabassum
ISBN: 978-93-5056-893-4
Edition: 2018
Published by: Discovery Publishing House Pvt. Ltd., New Delhi (India)

Rapid Eye Movement Sleep
Past and Future

Dr. Sangeeta Singh

ABSTRACT

Sleep is defined as a reversible behavioural state of perceptual disengagement from and unresponsiveness to the environment (Carskadon and Dement, 1989). It is a natural process known to occur in all mammals and birds studied so far. It is a complex and mysterious phenomenon. Earlier sleep was regarded as passive phenomenon caused by fatigue or cessation of continuous sensory inflows assailing the brain during wakefulness. Studies performed by Nauta, 1946 implicated the active generation of sleep. After the discovery of REM sleep, sleep has been divided into two separate states namely - non rapid eye movement sleep (NREM sleep) and REM sleep. Each stage is characterized by a distinct set of physiological and behavioural features. These two states of sleep alternate with each other during each night's sleep. After the discovery of REM sleep, search for the structural and chemical substrates for the initiation and maintenance of REM sleep started. Many studies were conducted - transection studies, lesion studies, unit studies, microdialysis studies etc. to elucidate the mechanism of REM sleep and control of transition of one state to the other in sleep wakefulness cycle.

Department of Zoology, Bareilly College, Bareilly
email: sangeetasingh6010@gmail.com

Despite of so many studies the initiation, maintenance and regulation of REM sleep are poorly understood. One thing is clear that many areas of the brain especially basal forebrain and pons varolli interact to regulate sleep wakefulness cycle. More studies have to be conducted in future to understand the mechanism of sleep generation.

INTRODUCTION

Sleep – wakefulness is a complex amalgam of physiological and behavioural process. Sleep is usually accompanied by postural recumbence, quiescence, closed eyes. It was first classified by Loomis *et al.*, 1937 based on EEG in humans. Earlier sleep was viewed as passive phenomenon caused by fatigue or cessation of continuous sensory inflows assailing the brain during wakefulness. This view was based on the experiments with transaction at upper brainstem level was followed by EEG synchronization (Bremer, 1935). Later on it was considered as an active phenomenon. The idea of active sleep was supported by experiments which showed that lesions of the anterior hypothalamus resulted in insomnia (Nauta, 1946).Within sleep; two states have been defined based on polygraphic measures of EEG, EMG and EOG. These states are –non rapid eye movement (NREM) sleep or slow wave sleep and rapid eye movement (REM) sleep. REM sleep was discovered by Aserinsky and Kleitman in 1953 which was characterized by eye movements and cortical activation. Other characteristics of REM sleep include muscle atonia, hippocampal theta rhythm, ponto-geniculo-occipital waves and myoclonic and cardiorespiratory fluctuations. It is the deepest stage of sleep and has also been termed paradoxical sleep, desynchronized sleep, active sleep and dream sleep.

Sleep has been shown to occur in all mammals and birds studied so far. In all the placental and marsupial mammals both slow wave sleep and REM sleep have been found. A REM sleep like state has been reported to occur in *Echidna* as well as in platypus (monotremes). The alteration of NREM with periods of REM sleep constitutes the sleep cycle which corresponds to basic rest and activity cycle (BRAC). The onset of sleep under normal circumstances in normal adult human is through NREM sleep. In human the average period of NREM-REM sleep cycle is approximately 90 min and 11 min in case of rats (Zeplin, 1989). In general, a human neonate sleeps for 16-17 hours per day after which sleep decreases with age.

Transection studies: Earlier studies (in 1960s) included the transection studies in which the brain was cut at different levels in order to grossly identify the area involved in the generation of REM sleep. It was established by Jouvet in 1972 that the structures necessary for the generation of REM sleep were localized within pons. When the brain was transected at the level of midbrain, all signs of REM sleep can be recorded caudal to the cut (Jouvet, 1972; Villablanca, 1966). In animals with brain stem transected between the medulla and pons (Siegel *et al.*, 1984, medulla and the rostral regions produced independent physiologically defined states. REM sleep signs were lost with further transection at the mid pontine level (Siegel, 1985).

Lesion studies: To further localize the regions within the pons necessary for REM sleep generation, lesion studies were done. Earlier studies supported the role of Locus Coeruleus in the generation of REM sleep (Jouvet and Delorme, 1965; Sastre *et al*, 1979). However, this could not be confirmed by other studies (Carli and Zenchetti, 1965; Jones, 1979). Friedman and Jones (1984) applied computer analysis and cluster analysis to investigate the effects of pontine tegmental radiofrequency lesions on sleep-wakefulness states. Their study suggested that the cells or fibers located within the lateral gigantocellular tegmental neurons and not locus coeruleus are important for the generation of REM sleep.

Unit studies: Guided by the transection and lesion studies, researchers have recorded single unit activity from pontine neurons which might be involved in REM sleep. Unit recording was done in many regions within the pons namely, medial pontine region, locus coeruleus, dorsolateral pontine region (LDT), PPT (Hobson *et al.*, 1975; Aston-Jones and

Bloom, 1981; Kayama *et al.*, 1992) etc. These studies showed that there are two types of neurons based on their activity during sleep-wakefulness cycle- REM-on and REM-off neurons. REM off (locus coeruleus neurons, serotonergic neurons) are those neurons which fire actively during wakefulness, slow down during NREM sleep and stop firing during REM sleep episode. REM - on neurons increase their firing rate in REM sleep for example LDT-PPT neurons. These neurons have been known to project diffusely to wide areas of the brain. Thus, it was concluded that neurons of LDT-PPT area may have a pivotal role in the initiation and generation of REM sleep.

NEUROTRANSMIITERS AND REM SLEEP

Much of the knowledge about the role of neurotransmitters in the regulation of REM sleep has come from pharmacological studies. The major neurotransmitters implicated to play role in the REM sleep are norepinephrine, acetylcholine, serotonin and GABA. Initially, norepinephrine was shown to have an important role in the generation of REM sleep. However, further finer studies could not confirm its role in generation but supported a permissive role for NE in the REM sleep. Serotonin (5-HT) has been shown to induce similar suppressive effects on REM sleep. This is suggested by the finding that reuptake inhibitors targeting primarily either NE or 5-HT transporters all suppress REM sleep in rats, cats and human (Hartmann *et al.*, 1971; Monti, 1983). Mild electrical stimulation of locus coeruleus neurons (NE-ergic) for 8 hours has been shown to reduce REM sleep in rats (Singh and Mallick, 1996) indicating that these neurons cease firing before a REM sleep episode. In other words, cessation of NE-ergic neurons locus coeruleus neurons is must for the REM sleep episode to begin.

In 1963, Hernandez-Peon *et al.* demonstrated that sleep like state could be induced by applying Ach crystals directly into the limbic forebrain- midbrain circuit of Nauta. Since then many investigators have shown that some or all parts of REM sleep state could be produced by direct administration of cholinergic agonists into pontine tegmentum, LDT-PPT, medial reticular formation and that Ach is essential to the generation of REM sleep (Jones, 1991). Endogenous cholinergic transmission enhanced by acetylcholinesterase inhibitors have shown to increase REM sleep. Microdialysis studies reported enhanced release of endogenous Ach in the medial PRF during natural REM sleep (Kodama *et al.*, 1990)

There are some neurotransmitters that modulate Ach release, thus influence the occurrence of REM sleep episode. GABA, as we all know is the main inhibitory neurotransmitter in the brain. Pharmacological studies using GABA antagonists have shown to increase Ach release resulting in the increase in REM sleep.

INTERACTION BETWEEN NEUROTRANSMITTERS FOR THE GENERATION OF REM SLEEP

It was shown that pharmacologically enhanced levels of Ach, produced by peripheral administration of serine, produced a state of wakefulness but the same drug produces a state of REM sleep when monoamines had previously depleted by reserpine (Karczmar *et al.*, 1970). These results revealed the potential importance of interplay between cholinergic and monoaminergic neurons in the control of REM sleep. Reciprocal interaction model was proposed by Hobson and coworkers in 1975. They stated that during waking, REM off neurons (NE-ergic or serotoninergic) is active and inhibit cholinergic REM - on neurons. During NREM sleep, REM - off neurons slows down their firing resulting in the withdrawal of the inhibition of REM - on neurons. Once activated, REM - on neurons initiates REM sleep. This model was revised in the light of further studies that identified pontine regions containing REM - on neurons (LDT-PPT area and medial pontine reticular formation). Small GABA containing neurons are also found in the region intermingled with cholinergic neurons and also near LC neurons. Interaction between REM - on and REM - off neurons could be possible via GABA-ergic interneuron. Hypocretins, discovered in 1998 and produced by hypothalamus are known to influence aminergic and cholinergic systems during sleep wake cycle. Under the influence of suprachaismatic neuron (SCN), hypothalamus produces hypocretins which cause wakefulness.

In the absence of excitatory stimuli from SCN, NREM sleep is initiated. During NREM sleep, LC neurons slow down their firing. This results in the liberation of cholinergic REM - on neurons from the inhibitory stimuli of LC neurons, resulting in the generation of a REM sleep episode.

Other neurotransmitter systems, namely GABA-ergic systems, dopaminergic systems, glutamatergic systems histaminergic systems and neuropeptidergic systems have been reported to play a role in the regulation of sleep/REM sleep by many studies done in the past and present.

CONCLUSION

Though numerous studies strongly support the role of cholinergic transmission in the regulation of REM sleep, neurochemically distinct systems interact in the regulation of sleep and wakefulness. Wakefulness is controlled by aminergic, cholinergnic and hypothalamic (hypocretins) systems. Pontine neurons along with the preoptic area control REM sleep and NREM sleep. Transition from one state to the other in sleep wakefulness seems to involve both mutual and reciprocal interactions between the controlling neurons. An understanding of these interactions is necessary to elucidate the mechanism of sleep generation especially REM sleep and to better understand the effects of drugs, injury and neurologic disease on sleep and wakefulness (Flavio-Aloe *et al.*, 2005).

FUTURE DIRECTIONS

The measurement of circulating neurotransmitters and those released locally in sleep generating areas should be characterized by more sensitive techniques. Typical microdialysis probe allows the diffusion of some of the compounds that have less molecular weight than the molecular cut- off weight of the probe into the lumen. REM sleep deprivation is followed by a rebound increase in REM sleep indicating the importance of REM sleep. Measurement of local neurotransmitter/s release during rebound REM sleep will greatly help to understand the mechanism of generation of REM sleep. Sensor technologies (use of biosensors) need improvements to develop better understanding of neurotransmitter release during sleep especially REM sleep.

REFERENCES

Carskadon, M.A. and Dement, W.C. (1989) Normal Human Sleep: An Overview. In: Principles and Practice of Sleep Medicine. M.H. Kryger, T. Roth and W.C. Dement, eds. Saunders, Philadelphia.

Nauta, W.J.H. (1946) Hypothalamic Regulation of Sleep in Rats. An Experimental Study. J. Neurophysiol. 9: 285-316.

Loomis, A.L., Harvery, E.N. and Hobart, G.A. (1937) Cerebral States during Sleep as Studied by Human Brain Potentials. J. Exp. Psychol. 21: 127-144.

Bremer, F. (1935) Cerveau 'isole' et physiologie du sommeil C.R. Soc. Biol. 118: 1235-1241.

Aserinsky E. and Kleitman, N. (1953) Regularly Occurring Periods of Eye Motility and Concomitant Phenomena during Sleep. Science 118: 273-274.

Zeplin, H. (1989) Mammalian Sleep In: Principles and Practice of Sleep Medicine. M.H. Kryger, T. Roth and W.C. Dement, eds. Saunders, Philadelphia, 30-40.

Jouvet, M. (1972) The Role of Monoamines in the Regulation of the Sleep-waking Cycle. Ergebn. Physiol. 64: 163-307.

Villablanca, J. (1966) Behavioural and Polygraphic Study of Sleep and Wafefulness in Chronic Decerebrate Cats. Electroencephalog. Clin. Neurophysiol. 21: 562-577.

Siegel, J.M., Nienhuis, R. Tomaszewski, K.S. (1984) REM Sleep Signs Rostral to Chronic Transections at the Pontomedullary Junction. Neurosci. Lett., 45: 241-246.

Siegel, J.M. (1985) Pontomedullary Interactions in the Generation of REM Sleep. In: Brain Mechanisms of Sleep, D.J. Mcginty, R.Drucker- Colin, A.R. Morrison and P.I. Permeggiani eds. Raven Press, New York, 157-154.

Jouvet, M. and Delorme, J.F. (1965) Locus coeruleus et sommeil paradoxical C.R. Soc. Biol. 159: 895-899.

Sastre, J.P., Sakai, K. and Jouvet, M. (1981) Are the gigantocellular tegmental Field neurons Responsible for Paradoxical Sleep? Brain Res. 229: 147-161.

Carli G. and Zanchetti, A. (1965) A Study of Pontine Lesions Suppressing Deep Sleep in the Cat. Arch. Ital. Biol. 103: 751-788.

Jones, B.E. (1979) Elimination of Paradoxical Sleep by Lesions of the Pontine Gigantocellular Tegmental Field in the Cat. Neurosci. Lett. 13: 285-293.

Friedman, L. and Jones, B.E. (1984) Computer Graphics Analysis of Sleep - Wakefulness State Changes after Pontine Lesions. Brain Res. Bull. 13: 53-68.

Hobson, J.A., McCarley, R.W. and Wyzinski, P.W. (1975) Sleep Cycle Oscillation: Reciprocal Discharge by Two Brainstem Neuronal Groups. Science, 189: 55-58.

Aston Jones, G. and Bloom, F.E. (1981) Norepinephrine Containing Locus Coeruleus Neurons in Behaving Rats Exhibit Pronounced Responses to Non-noxious Environmental Stimuli. J. Neurosci., 1: 887-900.

Kayama, Y., Ohta, M. and Jodo, E. (1992) Firing of Possibly Cholinergic Neurons in the Rat Laterotegmental Nucleus during Sleep and Wakefulness. Brain Res. 569: 210-220.

Hartmann, E. Bridwell, T.J. and Schildkraut, J.J. (1971) Alpha Methylparatyrosine and Sleep in the Rat Psychopharmacol. 21: 157-164.

Monti, J.M. (1983) Catecholamines and the Sleep Wake Cycle. II REM Sleep. Life Sci., 32: 1401-1415.

Singh, S. and Mallick, B.N. (1996) Mild Electrical Stimulation of Pontine Tegmentum Around locus coeruleus Reduces Rapid Eye Movement Sleep in Rats. Neuroscience Research, 24, 227-235.

Jones, B.E. (1991) Paradoxical Sleep and its Chemical/Structural Substrates in the Brain. Neuoscience, 40: 637-656.

Hernandez- Peon, R., Chavez-Ibbara, G., Morgane P.J. and Timo-Iaria, C. (1963) Limbic Cholinergic Pathways Involved in Sleep and Emotional Behaviour. Exp. Neurol. 8: 93-111.

Kodama, T., Takahashi, Y. and Honda, Y. (1990) Enhancement of Acetylcholine Release during Paradoxical Sleep in the Dorsal Tegmental Field of the Cat Brain Stem. Neurosci. Lett. 114: 277-282.

Karczmar, A.G., Longo, V.G. and De Carolis, A.S. (1970) A Pharmacological Model of Paradoxical Sleep: The Role of Cholinergic and Monoamine Systems. Physiol. Behav. 5: 175-182.

Flavio-Aloe, Alexandre Pinto de Azevedo and Rosa Hasan (2005) Sleep-wake Cycle Mechanisms. Rev. Bras. Psiquiatr. Vol. 27 suppl. 1.

Pages: 19-27

Renewable Resources and Environment

Edited by: Dr. Baby Tabassum

ISBN: 978-93-5056-893-4

Edition: 2018

Published by: Discovery Publishing House Pvt. Ltd., New Delhi (India)

A Review of Ill Effects of Arsenic on Human Health and Fishes and its Remediation

Robeena Sarah; Baby Tabassum
Priya Bajaj and Nida Idrees

ABSTRACT

The paper reviews the prevalence of contamination of arsenic (As) in food, soil and water. It occurs both naturally and as result of pollution. Concentrations of inorganic arsenic is high in air close to industrial sources, in underground water, in areas with natural geological contamination. Concentrations of organic arsenic is high in sea food. Inorganic arsenic being generally considered more toxic. Human population is mostly exposed to arsenic through ingestion, inhalation and dermal contact. Drinking water is the primary and main route of exposure to arsenic. Consumption of the arsenic contaminated fishes collected from the polluted waters might also contribute to bioaccumulation of arsenic in human beings. Depending on the span & severity of arsenic exposure, it may be Chronic or Acute. Acute arsenic exposure produces toxicity of liver, kidney, intestine and brain. Chronic ingestion of high dose of inorganic arsenic in drinking water causes multisystem adverse health effects. The fishes have been found to be particularly susceptible to As toxicity when they were continually exposed to it. The action of *Azadirachta indica* as a remedy for controlling the ill-effects of arsenic has been

Toxicology Laboratory, Department of Zoology, Govt. Raza P.G. College, Rampur (U.P.) (India)

recognized. A Non-toxic, monetary profitable and herbal remedy against arsenic toxicity would have been proposed to the fish farmers.

Keywords: Arsenic, Human health, fishes, *Azadirachta indica*.

INTRODUCTION

Increased industrialization, heavy population and urbanization growth created a serious threat to all kinds of life in the form of pollution which has now become a global problem. Among all types of pollution, aquatic pollution is of greater concern as each and every kind of the life depends on water (Ananth & Mathivanan, 2013). Among the aquatic pollutants, heavy metals are of greatest concern. Heavy metals after reaching the aquatic bodies deteriorate the life, sustaining the quality of water and cause damages to both flora and fauna. The problem increases many folds due to their long half-life period and properties of non-biodegradability, bioaccumulation and biomagnifications.(Verma *et.al.*, 2005).

Arsenic, a toxic metalloid, is prevalent in the environment, where it occurs both naturally and as result of pollution. Inorganic arsenic being generally considered more toxic. Concentrations of inorganic arsenic is high in air close to industrial sources, in underground water in areas with natural geological contamination, water bodies near dumping sites of Electrical & Electronic Equipments Waste and in soils or sediments near contamination sources. Concentrations of organic arsenic is particularly high in sea-living animals and therefore in seafood. It is a well-documented human carcinogen and, is a naturally occurring metalloid present in food, soil and water. Global natural emission of arsenic and its compounds has been estimated to be 8000 tons per year while emission from man-made sources is about three times higher at 23,600 tons per year.

In India, around 80% of the rural population and 50% of the urban population use ground water for domestic purposes. Water quality issues like arsenic, salinity, nitrate, iron, flouride and heavy metals in water due to geogenic and anthropogenic reasons have been reported from various parts of the country. High arsenic content in ground water affects the human, animal, soil and plant systems. As many as 96 districts in 12 States have been affected by high arsenic contamination in ground water. 70.4 million people in 35 districts alone have been exposed to groundwater arsenic. Over one lakh deaths and 2 to 3 lakhs of confirmed cases of illness have reportedly been caused by groundwater arsenic.

ARSENIC AFFECTED REGIONS

Arsenic contamination in drinking water has become a significant concern in Bangladesh, West Bengal (India), China, Mongolia, Nepal, Cambodia, Myanmar, Afghanistan, Korea, and Pakistan (Mukherjee *et al.* 2004). Arsenic contamination is highly prevalent in various regions in India. High level of Arsenic in ground water has been found in the states of Bihar, Uttar Pradesh, Jharkhand, Assam, Tripura, Arunachal Pradesh, Nagaland, Manipur, Chhattisgarh and Andhra Pradesh. Arsenic poisoning was first detected in West Bengal in July, 1983 (Mukherjee *et al.*, 2006). Like other heavy metals like Iron, Cadmium, Copper etc, Arsenic was found in Gomti River originating in Uttar Pradesh (Kumar *et al.*, 2013). States in the region of the upper, middle and lower Ganga and Brahmaputra plain are most affected by arsenic (Chakraborti *et al.*, 2003).

SOURCES OF ARSENIC EXPOSURE

Exposure to arsenic via occupational & environmental sources represents a major health concern worldwide according to the WHO (WHO, 2001). Different forms of arsenic are used in the treatment of timber, in agriculture, ceramic, glass, semiconductor and pharmaceutical industry, refining of metallic ores, smelting of metals, burning of fossil fuels, pesticide manufacturing, semiconductor etc. Arsenic is one of the most important toxicant present as gallium arsenide found in LEDs, solar cells, microwaves, semi-conductors, circuit boards, LCD displays and computer chips. However, human arsenic exposure may also come from hazardous waste sites.

Exposure to this dangerous element generally occurs by ingestion, inhalation, through direct dermal contact or may be transmitted from the mother to the foetus via the placental route (Tchounwou *et al.*, 2003). Ingestion of low dose via food or water is the main pathway of this metalloid into the organism, where absorption takes place in the stomach and intestines, followed by release into the bloodstream. Only very high exposure can, in fact, lead to appreciable accumulation in the body. Minor alternative pathways of entry are known through inhalation and dermal exposure."(Caroli *et.al.*,1996). Consumption of the arsenic contaminated fishes collected from the polluted waters might also contribute to bioaccumulation of arsenic in human beings.

ARSENIC IN THE ENVIRONMENT

Human population is mostly exposed to arsenic through ingestion, inhalation and dermal contact. Ingestion of arsenic contaminated water, foods, drugs, wines, smoke of cigarette and fossil fuels are the various routes of arsenic exposure to the population both acute and chronically (NTP, 1999). In occupational exposure, the workers are exposed to airborne arsenic from the industries of smelting and refining metals, producing and using arsenic-containing chemicals, manufacturing of glass, semiconductors and various pharmaceutical substances (USPHS, 1989). Arsenic is present in sea food in its organic form with elevated concentration, which are considerably less toxic than inorganic arsenic (ATSDR, 1998). Drinking water is the primary and main route of exposure to arsenic. MCL is the standard concentration of arsenic in drinking water which is not hazardous, is set by the USEPA that is 10 µg/l (EPA, 2001) and the guideline value for concentration of arsenic in drinking water is recommended by the WHO is also 10 µg/l (WHO, 1992).

HUMAN HEALTH EFFECTS

Depending on the span & severity of arsenic exposure, it may be Chronic or Acute. Acute arsenic exposure produces toxicity of liver, kidney, intestine and brain. Chronic ingestion of inorganic arsenic causes multisystem adverse health effects.

High dose of arsenic in drinking water causes characteristic skin manifestation, vascular disease including arteriosclerosis [Peripheral vascular disease and ischemic heart disease (ISHD), renal disease, neurological effects, cardiovascular disease, chronic lung disease, cerebrovascular disease, reproductive effects and cancers of skin,lungs, liver, kidney and bladder. Increased exposure of arsenic is also associated with non insulin dependent diabetes mellitus (Rahman *et al.*, 1998; Wang *et al.*, 2003). Chronic arsenical dermatosis arises from consuming arsenic contaminated drinking water for long time. Liver is the target organ of arsenic toxicity, showing the detoxification role of the liver (Mormede & Davies, 2001). As the principal metabolic organ, liver plays a major role in uptake, accumulation, biotransformation & excretion of arsenic (Pedlar & Klaverkamp,2002). In chronic poisoning, arsenic is then converted by the liver to a less toxic form, from where it is eventually largely excreted in the urine.

EFFECTS ON FISHES

Fish is a major and easily available source of food in nature for mankind. It provides a significant amount of animal protein intake in the diet of a large population. It has been advised that fish should be consumed two or three times weekly because of the pharmaceutical effects of omega 3 polyunsaturated fatty acids which exist abundantly in fish oil. But, wide ranges of contaminants are continuously introduced into the aquatic environments and fish from polluted waters seriously threaten human health due to the bioaccumulation of metals in muscle and other tissues. Fish, as a living bio indicator organism, play an increasingly important role in monitoring of water pollution since they respond with great sensitivity to changes in the aquatic environment (Santhananm *et.al.*,1987). Once these toxic substance enters into body, they damage and weaken the mechanism concerned leading to physiological, pathological and biochemical disorders (Braunbeck & Segnor, 1992). Fishes are very sensitive to a change in their environment and can play significant role in assessing potential risk associated with contamination in aquatic environment (Lakra and Nagpure, 2009). The studies carried out on various fishes have shown that heavy metals may alter the physiological activities and biochemical parameters both in tissues and in blood (Vinodhini and Narayanan, 2008). When spotted snakehead (*Channa punctatus*, Bloch) fishes were exposed to high concentration (2 mM) of sodium arsenite (NaAsO), they died within 2.5 hr. The fishes have been found to be particularly susceptible to As toxicity when they were continually exposed to it through gills and intake of As contaminated food (Ahmed *et al.*, 2008).

HERBAL REMEDIATION TO REDUCE ARSENIC TOXICITY

Existing treatment Protocols are insufficient to tackle the widespread Arsenic toxicity. The clinical importance of herbal drugs has gained popularity. Thus an alternative & safe option is required to combat this problem. Neem (*Azadirachta indica*) is one of the most popular, auspicious and well-known tree which is more extensively studied for its pharmaceutical and clinical properties. It is a tropical evergreen tree native to India and is also found in other southeast countries. Since the last few years neem is getting extraordinary popularity across the world. It is called a 'domestic doctor' in India due to its common availability and wide efficacy. The role of neem tree in controlling water, air and land pollution is wonderful. Neem is a natural resource to keep the environment clean and healthy. It possesses a number of pharmacological activities. The seeds, barks and leaves contain compounds with proven antiseptic, antiviral, antipyretic, anti-inflammatory, anti-fungal and anti-ulcer uses. Due to antioxidant activity of Neem, it has been used to cure oxidative damage to liver, kidney and other organs of the body against arsenic toxicity. Therefore, Neem deserves to be called as "Wonder plant".

CONCLUSION

Arsenic, a reactive metalloid is one of the most important and concerned global environment toxicant. It is wide spread in the environment as a result of both geogenic processes and anthropogenic disturbances (Bear *et al.*, 2006). Exposure to arsenic may come from natural source, from industrial source, or from administered acute poisoning. Ingestion via food or water is the main pathway of arsenic into the organism. Fish have long been used as sentinels for biomonitoring of aquatic environmental pollutants and are good indicators of arsenic toxicity (Tistler *et.al.*, 2002). Humans are more sensitive to arsenic than animals. No medicine was found effective once complication developed. Arsenic free water or environment or decrease in arsenic concentration level is only the solution of arsenicosis. A Non-toxic, monetary profitable and herbal remedy against arsenic toxicity would have been proposed to the fish farmers. Cheaper means for the treatment of arsenic toxicity in the fish inhabiting in the contaminated regions will be established. The action of *Azadirachta indica* as a remedy for controlling the ill-effects of arsenic has been recognized.

REFERENCES

Ahmed, K., Akhand, A.A., Hasan, M., Islam, M. and Hasan, A. (2008): Toxicity of Arsenic (Sodium Arsenite) to Fresh Water Spotted Snakehead *Channa punctatus* (Bloch) on Cellular Death and DNA Content. *Am-Euras. J. Agric. Environ. Sci.*, 4(1): 18-22.

Ananth S. and Mathivanan V., (2013). Studies on Biochemical Changes in the Fish *Ctenopharyngodon idella* in Relation to Arsenic Toxicity. International Journal of Pharmaceutical & Biological Archives, 2013; 4(6): 1226-1232.

ATSDR, Agency for Toxic Substances and Disease Registry (1998): Toxicological Profile for Arsenic (update). U.S. Public Health Service, U. S., DHHS, Atlanta, GA.

Bear, H., Richards, J.G. and Schulte, P.M. (2006): Arsenic Exposure Alters Heptic Arsenic Species Composition and Stress-mediated Gene Expression in the Common Killifish (*Fundulus heteroclitus*). Aquatic. Toxical 77: 257-266.

Braunbeck, T. and Segnor, H. (1992). Pre-exposure, Temperature, Acclimation and Diet as Modifying Factors for the Tolerance of Golden ide *(leuciscus idus melanotus)* to Short Time Exposure to 4-chloroaniline. *Eco toxology and Enveionmental Safety*, 24: 72-94.

Caroli, F. Torre, LA. Petrucci, F. and Violante, N (1996). Element Speciation in Bioinorganic Chemistry, Edited by Sergio Caroli, *Chemical Analysis Series*, 135, pp. 445-463.

Chakraborti, D., Mukherjee, S.C., Pati, S., Sengupta, M.K., Rahman, M.M., Chowdhury, U.K., Lodh, D., Chanda, C.R., Chakraborti, A.K., Basu, G.K. (2003): Arsenic Groundwater Contamination in Middle Ganga Plain, Bihar, India: A Future Danger? *Environ. Health Perspect.*, 111(9): 1194 1201.

Environmental Protection Agency (EPA), Federal Register, 66(14) (2001): National Primary Drinking Water Regulations; Arsenic and Clarification to Compliance and New Source Contaminations Monitoring; Final Rule (January 22, 2001).

Kumar, D., Verma, A., Dhusia, N., More, N. (2013): Water Quality Assessment of River Gomti in Lucknow. *Univ. J. Environ. Res. Technol.*, 3(3): 337-344.

Lakra, W.S. and Nagpure, N.S. (2009): Genotoxicological Studies in Fishes. A Review. Indian Journal of Animal Science. 79: 93-98.

Mormede, S., and Davies, I. (2001): Heavy Metal Concentrations in Commercial Deep Sea Fish from the Rockall Trough. Continental Shelf Research. 21: 899-916.

Mukherjee, S., Das, D., Darbar, S., Mukherjee, M., Das, A.S. and Mitra, C. (2004): Arsenic Trioxide Generates Oxidative Stress and Islet Cell Toxicity in Rabbit. *Current Science*, 86, 854-858.

Mukherjee, A., Sengupta, M.K., Hossain, M.A., Ahamed, S., Das, B., Haematological Nayak, B., Lodh, D., Rahman, M.M., Chakraborti, D. (2006): Arsenic Contamination in Groundwater: A Global Perspective with Emphasis on the Asian Scenario. *J. Health, Popul. Nutr.*, 24(2): 142 163.

NTP, National Toxicological Program (1999): Arsenic and Certain Arsenic Compound. In: Eighth Report on Carcinogens: 1998 Summery. U.S. Public Health Service, U.S., DHHS, Atlanta, GA. pp. 17-19.

Rahman, M., Tondel, M., Ahmad, S.A. and Axelson, O. (1998): Diabetes Mellitus Associated with Arsenic Exposure in Bangladesh. Am. J. Epidemiol., 148, 198-203.

Santhananm R, Sukumaran N and Natarajan P.A. (1987). Manual of Fresh Water Aquaculture. Oxford and FBH Publishing Co. Pvt. Ltd., New Delhi-2.

Tistler, T. and Zagorc, J.(2002): Acute & Chronic Toxicity of Arsenic to some Aquatic Organisms. Bull. Env. Cont. Toxicol. 69: 421-429.

Tchounwou, P.B., Patlolla, A.K., Centeno, J.A. (2003): Carcinogenic and Systemic Health Effects Associated with Arsenic Exposure a Critical Review. Toxicol. Pathol., 31: 575-588.

USPHS, (1989). Toxicological Profile for Arsenic. Washington, DC: US Public Health Servia.

Verma R.S., Khan M.A., Tripathi R., Shukla S. and Sharma U.D. (2005): Heavy Metal Toxicity to Fresh Water Prawn, Macrobrachium Dayanum (Crustacea-Decapoda). *Aquacult., 6(1),* 57-62.

Vinodhini, R. and Narayanan, M. (2008): Bioaccumulation of Heavy Metals in Organs of Fresh Water Fish *Cyprinus carpio* (Common carp). *Int. J. Environ. Sci. Tech.,* 5(2): 179-182.

Wang, S.E., Chiou, J.M., Chen, C.J., Tseng, C.H., Chou, W.L., Wang, C.C., Wu, T.N. and Chang, L.W. (2003): Prevalence of Non-Insulin-Dependent Diabetes Mellitus and Related Vascular Disease in Southwestern Arsenicosis-endemic and Non Endemic Areas in Taiwan. Environ. Hlth. Perspect., 111, 155-159.

WHO (1992): Guideline for Drinking Water Quality, Recommendation, Vol. 1. 2nd Edn. Geneva: World Health Organization. p. 41.

***Pages:* 28-43**

Renewable Resources and Environment
***Edited by:* Dr. Baby Tabassum**
ISBN: 978-93-5056-893-4
***Edition:* 2018**
***Published by:* Discovery Publishing House Pvt. Ltd., New Delhi (India)**

Effect of Arsenic on Certain Biochemical Parameters in Liver Tissue of an Air Breathing Fish *Channa Gachua*

Qaisur Rahman[1] and Baby Tabassum[2]

ABSTRACT

Fishes are primary aquatic vertebrates using gills for respiration, changes of water qualities such as pH, dissolved oxygen, toxicity and amount of toxic compounds and are some of the major causes of respiratory distress to fish with relatively high level of environmental stressors.The effect of heavy metal toxicant on enzymatic activity is one of the most important biochemical parameters which are affected under stress. The environment is currently polluted by thousands of chemicals or xenobiotic introduced into the environment by man to meet the demands of the modern era. The pollution is continuous and alarming influx to aquatic environment worldwide from both naturally occurring and anthropogenic sources. The polluted water may lead to the destruction of the beneficial species either directly effecting aquatic forms of life in directly through breaking the biological food chain such as fish and their habitat and behavioral pattern. The fish as a bio indicator of aquatic medium it plays an important

[1] Dept. of Zoology, Vinoba Bhave University, Hazaribagh, Pin - 825 301 (Jharkhand) (India)

[2] Dept. of Zoology, Govt Raza, Post Graduate College, Rampur, Pin - 244 901 (U.P.) (India)

email: qaisur.rahman@gmail.com

role in the monitoring of water pollution because of the sudden death of fish indicates heavy pollution and the effects of exposure to sub lethal levels can be measured in terms of biochemical, physiological and histological responses of the fishes. In the present study, the sub lethal effects of arsenic on various biochemical parameters of *Channa gachua* were studied. The fish was exposed to sub lethal concentration of arsenic for 20 days for chronic toxicity studies. In the present study total protein, amino acid and acetylcholinesterase, glycogen and lactic acid were observed. The present study showed the protein content was decreased and amino acid content was increased significantly and also Acetylcholinesterase was increased in the liver tissue of arsenic treated fish, *Channa gachua*. The present study shows the level of glycogen decreased and lactic acid increased in the liver tissue of fish exposed to arsenic. These changes were concentration dependent. The details will be discussed in this paper.

Keywords: Biochemical parameters, Arsenic, Liver, *Channa gachua*.

INTRODUCTION

Arsenic is a trace element and it under goes multiple electron transfer reactions. Arsenic exists in soluble and insoluble forms, organic and inorganic trivalent and pentavalent forms among which the trivalent arseniteis highly toxic. It occurs in the earth's crust along with sulphides and iron pyrites. The sources of arsenic found in environment includes natural and manmade. It is released into the human environment including drinking water through the mining and burning coal, smelting of copper and through industrial effluents. Qaisur and Sadhu (2012) reported that chemicals containing arsenic are also used in the manufacturing of herbicides and pesticides, leads shots and phosphate detergents and in preservation of wood and hide. Arsenical herbicides and pesticides applied to agricultural soils and vegetation also may be important sources of arsenic contamination of food stuffs respectively. Arsenic is a toxic element for humans and it is commonly associated with serious health disruptions Brookes (1998). Total diet as studies carried out in various countries have shown that fish and shell fish are the most significant dietary source of as, accounting for nearly three quarters of total intake Dokkum *et al.,* (1989) and Tao *et al.,* (1999). The concentration of as was found in environmental samples, mainly in waters where inorganic form is predominant (Smith *et al.,* 2000, Elci *et al.,* 2008). Arsenic exposure has been related to the appearance of some types of cancer Ranbis *et al.,* (2003). A report on an assessment of the cancer risk associated with consumption of oysters caused a panic among consumers in Taiwan Guo (2002). Some of these human health effects currently observed in population of South and Southeastern Asia, particularly in countries such as Bangladesh and India AlRamali (2005). Besides the direct exposure of humans as through drinking contaminated water, this might also be biologically available to aquatic organisms, such as fish which are used as human food there by providing an additional source of nutrition. Arsenic has a considerable tendency to accumulate in bottom sediments Svobodovo (2002). For this reason, issues related to as content in aquatic organisms and sea fish in particular, have attracted considerable attentions. The relevance of this as intake will depend on the concentration of accumulated by the fish Lai *et al.,* (2001). During recent years, serious concern has been voiced about the rapidly deteriorating state of fresh water bodies with respect to toxic metals pollution. Fishes are often at the top of the aquatic food chain and accumulate large amounts of some metals from the water Tuzen (2003). Water pollution leads to fish contamination with toxic metals from many sources such as industrial and domestic wastewater, natural runoff and contributory rivers Rashed, (2001) Tariq *et al.,* (1991). Fishes, living in polluted water may accumulate toxic trace metals via their food chains; they assimilate metals by ingestion of particulate material suspended in water, ion exchange of dissolved metals across lipophilic membranes, e.g., the gills, adsorption on tissue and membranes surfaces Alam *et al.,* (2002). The bioaccumulation of metals is therefore, an index of the pollution status of the relevant water body Mastoi *et al.*, (2008). Protein is the most important and abundant biochemical constituent present in the animal body. Hence, Proteins are important in all biological systems.

Protein and amino acids are very important nutrients. Protein plays a major role in the synthesis of microsomal detoxifying enzymes and helps to detoxify the toxicants which enter into the animal body Ramasamy (1987). Amino acids are the building blocks of protein which are organic compounds, meaning that they contain carbon and hydrogen bonded to each other. In addition to those two elements, they include nitrogen oxygen andin a few cases sulfur. The basic structure of an amino acid molecule consists of a carbon atom bonded to an amino group which is the (-NH2), a carboxyl group (-COOH) a hydrogen atom, and a fourth group that differs from one amino acid to another and often is referred to as the -Rgroup or the side chain. The R-group, which can vary widely, is responsible for the differences in chemical properties fetus Sankarsamipillai and Jagadeesan (2006). Acetylcholine sterase is an enzyme present in various tissues, including muscle and red cells, that breaks down acetylcholine a chemical released by nerves that activates muscle contractions and helps to maintain proper transmission of impulses between nerve cells and between nerve cells and muscles; also called true choline sterase. Measuring acetylcholine sterase in amniotic fluid may help confirm a suspected neural tube defect in the foetus Sankarsamipillai and Jagadeesan (2006). Carbohydrate is an essential energy source for all vital activities of an organism. It is stored in the form of glycogen in animals. Glycogen is broken down into glucose for energy requirements. The stressful condition disturbs the metabolic rate of carbohydrate and thus the level of glycogen; glucose and lactic acid are altered Srivastava and Singh (1980) and Metelev *et al.*, (1983); Qaisur and Shamim (2014) respectively. The present study was carried with an aim to investigate the sub lethal effect of arsenic in biochemical parameters in liver tissue of an air breathing fish *Channa gachua*.

MATERIALS AND METHODS

Live specimens of *Channa gachua* were procured from local fish dealers at Hazaribag (Latitude 25° 59′N and Longitude 85° 22′E) and maintained in large glass aquaria size (90×60×60cm) with continuous flow of water. The specimens were fed on chopped goat liver daily during a minimum acclimation period of 20 days in the laboratory. Routine oxygen consumption from air and still water was measured in a closed glass respirometer containing 3 litres of water (initial O_2 content = 6.5 mg O_2/litre; pH = 7.2) and 0.51 mL of air. The fish were acclimated to the respirometers for at least 12 hours before the readings were taken. The experiments were conducted at 29.0 ± 1.5°C. The pH of the ambient water was measured by an electronic pH meter systronics. The respiratory chambers were thermostated by immersion in a temperature controlled water bath. Fishes from 70-100 grams were used during the experiment. They were checked thoroughly for injury and disease conditions and only healthy fishes were used for this study. After washing with 0.01% $KMnO_4$ solution for 15 min, they were placed in nine plastic pools (300 L) containing non chlorinated water. Prior to the start of the experiment the fishes were acclimatized to the food and laboratory conditions with 12 hours dark and 12 hours light cycles. Fishes were divided into five equal groups each comprising of 30 fishes. Each group was kept in separate aquarium tanks. The first group was kept as negative control; the fishes were maintained in water containing normal water without any treatment. The fishes of two groups were exposed to a sub lethal concentration of 1 ppm concentration of Arsenic added in the water for 30 days respectively. Solutions were renewed once daily after exposure period, animals were sacrificed and the liver tissues were removed, homogenized and stored at –80 °C for further biochemical analysis. Protein content in the tissue was estimated by the method of Lowry *et al.,* (1951). Total free amino acids and content of the tissue were estimated by the method of Moore and Stein (1954). The enzyme acetylcholine sterase was assayed by Metcalf (1951). The glycogen content was estimated by Kemp and Kits Van Heijhingen (1954) and Lactic acid was done by the method of Barker and Summerson (1941). The data were subjected to student "t" test to find out the significance of difference between controland treated values.

RESULTS

In *Channa gachua* the gills are pinkish red in colour. Each gill arch is made up of two primary gill filaments. The filaments are beset with the secondary gill lamellae. The gills receive blood from the afferent branchial artery near the origin of gill lamellae. The opening of efferent branchial artery is situated just below the afferent branchial artery. The transverse ligament present between the both arteries. The secondary gill lamellae are covered by epithelial layer, which is made up of simple cuboidal cells, endowed with numerous mucous cells and acidophilic cells by Qaisur Rahman (2011). In the present study, attempts have been made to investigate the effects of sub lethal concentration of arsenic on various biochemical parameters of *Channa gachua* in acute and toxicity studies. In the liver tissue of control groups, the protein content was 86.92±1.98 mg/g wt. wt. of tissue. After the mercury exposure the level of protein content was significantly decreased in liver tissue of arsenic exposed fish, as compared to respective control levels (Table 4.1) shows the amino acid content in the brain tissue of fish. The level of protein content was increased in arsenic exposed fish. In the liver tissue of control fish, the acetylcholine sterase activity was 45.72±0.95 moles of acetylcholine hydrolysedper mg of protein/hr. During the arsenic exposure the activity of acetylcholine sterase was decreased in the liver tissue of fish. The level of glycogen content in the liver tissue of control fish was 11.99±1.96 mg/g wet wt. of tissue. During the arsenic exposure the level of glycogen decreased in the liver tissue (8.42±0.97mg/g wet wt. of tissue) in the liver tissue of control groups respectively. The lactic acid content was 2.84±1.08 mg/g weight of tissue. After the arsenic exposure the level of lactic acid content was significantly decreased in liver tissue of arsenic exposed fish, as compared to respective control levels.

Table 4.1

Showing biochemical parameters in liver tissue of *Channa gachua* treated with Arsenic

Parameters	Control	20 days Treated
Protein(mg/g)	86.92±1.98	73.85±1.68*
Amino acid (mg/g)	2.85±1.54	3.66±1.87*
Acetyl cholinesterase (AChE)	45.72±0.95	36.14±1.92*
Glycogen	11.99±1.96	8.42±0.97*
Lactic acid	2.84±1.08	4.22±1.87*

Mean ±S.D of six individual observations
*significance at 5% level

DISCUSSION

In the present study a reduction in the protein content observed in *Channa gachua* exposed with arsenic. These results suggest that the tissue protein undergoes proteolysis results in an increase in the production of free amino acids. These aminoacids are utilized for energy production during stressful situation in the intoxicated fishes. Neff (1985) has reported that decline in protein contentmay also be related to increased energy cost of homeostasis, tissue repair and detoxification during stress. In the present investigation sublethal concentrations of arsenic exposed fish *Channa gachua* exposed with arsenic show a decrease in protein content and an increase in amino acid content of liver for 20 days exposure of arsenic. Many investigations have also reported such achange in total protein content of various tissues in different fishes exposed to different heavy metals Rajamanikam (1992) Pazhanisamy (2002). Janaand Bandyopadhyay (1981) have reported such are duction in protein content when the fish *Channapunctatus* has been exposed to heavy metals suchas mercury, arsenic and lead. Protein depletion has been reported in the liver of *Anabas testudineus* exposed to nickel chloride Jha and Jha (1995). Decrease in the liver protein level is reported in the fish *Labeo rohita* exposed to arsenic Pazhanisamy (2002) *Channa punctatus* exposed to zinc andphenyl mercuric acetate Sen *et al.,* (1992) Karuppasamy (2000) *Channa punctatus* exposed to arsenic Jatyajit Hota, (1996) *Channa striatus* exposed to mercury cadmium and lead Palanichamy and Baskaran, (1995) and *Cirrhinamrigala* exposed to lead acetate Ramalingam *et al.,* (2000). Baskaran *et al.* (1991) have reported the impact of commercial detergent Nirma on feeding energetics and protein metabolism in the freshwater teleost fish *Oreochromis mossambicus*. The decrease in liver and muscle protein has been reported in the sugar mill effluent treated *Channa punctatus* after 96 hours exposure Avash Maruthi and Ramakrishna (2000). In the present investigation, the decreased level of proteinin brain tissue shows that fish exposed to arsenicare subject to stress. Similar results have also been recorded in the protein content of different tissues when the animals are exposed to various pollutants Palanichamy *et al.,* (1989) Malla Reddy and Bashamohideen (1988) Manoharan and Subbiah (1982) respectively. Meenakshi and Indra (1998) have noticed depletion in the level of total protein in liver and muscle and an increase in the total free amino acids in blood, liver and muscle of distillery effluent treated *Mystus vittatus*. The remarkable increase in the free amino acid may represent proteolysis in the tissues to meet the demands for energy requisites in addition to the carbohydrates and fat. Increase in amino acid content in liver is observed in *Mystus vittatus* exposed to median lethal concentration of mercuric chloride Jagdeesan (1994) and in *Mystus vittatus* exposed to sublethal and median lethal concentration of copper Rajamanickam (1992).

Anuradha and Raju (1996) have observed the increased level of amino acid content in liver, muscle, kidney and gill tissues of *Anabas scandens* exposed to selenium toxicity. The FAA serves as metabolites for a TCA cycle which have a key role in stepping up the energy requirement respectively.

Acetylchollinesterase (AchE) activity measurement in fish has been used for monitoring the neurotoxicity of pesticide Bretaud *et al.,*(2000). AchE, a serine hydrolase catalyzes the breakdown of the neurotransmitter acetylcholine into acetate and choline. This process involves the formation of a substrate enzyme complex, followed by acetylation of the hydroxyl group, the aminoacid serine, present within the Eastertic side andfinally deacetylation. The inhibitory effect on AchE activity indicates that pollutants like insecticide might interfere in the vital processes like energy metabolism of nervecells Nath and Kumar(1999). In the present study, 15 days exposure period of lead has resulted the inhibition of AchE activity level in the brain of *Channa gachua* a decrease in AchE activity level has led to the accumulation of acetylcholinein the brain of fish Josh *et al.,* (1982). AchE inhibition and an accumulation of ACh in the tissues of sumithion treated fish *Channa gachua* have been observed by Koundinya and Ramamurthi (1978). Bashamohideen and Sailbala (1989) have observed a steep decline inAchE activity with a concomitant elevation in AchEcontent in different tissues like gill, kidney, brain, liver and different types of muscles in *Cyprinuscarpio* following 10 days exposure to malathion. The decrease in brain AchE is found to be inversely proportional to the increase in Achcontent in methyl parathion treated tadpoles offrog, *Rana cyanophiclits*. Accumulation of Achand inhibition of AchE activity levels in liver, muscle, gill and brain have been reported in *Channa gachua* exposed to fenvalerate Ghosh, (1990). Ravi and Selvarajan (1990) have reported an increase in the levels of amine in the brain region of *Labeo rohita* and *Cyprinus carpio* exposed to phosalone. Sevgiler *et al.,* (2004) have reported a significant correlation between increase in lipid peroxidation and inhibition of AchE activity inliver. They have further stated that etoxazole mediated lipid peroxidation may be related to itsanticholine esterase action. Increased lipidperoxidation caused by etoxazole indicates that this compound induces the generation of reactive oxygen species, creating oxidative damage in the cell membrane. Yang and Dettab (1996) in their study with disisopropyl fluoro phosphates have suggested that AchE inhibitor induced cholinergic hyperactivity has initiated the accumulation of free radicals leading to lipid peroxidation, which may be the initiator of AchE inhibitor induced cell injury. Nachmanson and Feld (1947) have reported that the animal dies when AchE activity of the brain is inhibited by 95 percent. Coppage *et al.*, (1975) have observed 79 percent reduction in AchE activity in the esturine fish *Lagodon rhomboids* exposed to 48 hours median lethal concentrations (92±g/L) of malathion. Carbohydrate is an essential energy source for all vital activities of an organism. It is stored in the form of glycogen in animals. Glycogen is broken down into glucose for energy requirements. The stressful condition disturbs the metabolic rate of carbohydrate and thus the level of glycogen; glucose and lactic acid are altered Srivastava and Singh, (1980) Metelev *et al.*, (1983). The toxic substances are absorbed into the body and transported to various organs through blood. The blood glucose is a sensitive biochemical indicator of stress. Investigator like Qaisur and Sadhu (2012) in *Channa gachua* reported that the Exposure of fishes to different types of toxic substance is known toelicit changes in the biochemical constituents and thereby altering the metabolic pathways. In the present study the level of glycogen content and lactic acid was increased in the liver tissue of fish exposed to arsenic. Changes in the glycogen level of liver have been noticed by many investigators. Mcleay and Brown (1975) have recorded a considerable decrease in glycogen content of bleached kraft pulp mill effluent. Baskaran *et al.*, (1989) have noticed the depletion on the hepatic glycogen content in *Oreochromis mossambicus* when exposed to textile dye effluent. Depletion in the glycogen content of liver and muscle has been observed in *Rasbora daniconius* exposed to pulp and paper mill effluent Vijayaran and Vasugi (1989). *Channa gachua* exposed to sublethal concentration of arsenic shows an overall increase in the blood glucose at all periods of exposure thereby indicating that the glycol genolysis takes place in the liver, where by the reserved glycogen is being slowly converted into glucose. The hyperglycemic condition in the present study correlated with the observations of some researcher's *viz.*, the juvenile Cohosalmon on *Oncorhynchus kisutch* treated with sub lethal concentration of neutralized unbleached kraft mill effluent Mcleay (1973). Similar results were made by Vijayram, and Vasugi (1989) in paper and pulpmill effluents. Similar elevated blood glucose levelshave been noticed in *Heteropneustes fossilis* exposed to textile mill effluent Nisha and Shukla (1986). Lactic acid is formed through glycolysis under anaerobic condition of glucose catabolism. In the present study it showed an increase in the lactic acid content of liver and blood at allthe hours of effluent treatment. Accumulation of lactic acid is more in liver and blood of fishes exposed to raw effluent. It is likely that the lactic acid formed in the muscle and other tissue during glycolysis, might have been transported to liver *via* blood accounting for the hyper lactamia in blood and liver. Because of the absence of the enzymeglucose 6-phosphatase in the muscle which is necessary for the conversion of lactic acid into glucose, the lactic acid produced in the tissue is transported to the liver through blood Ambikashanmugam (1980). Since liver is the metabolicsite the lactic acid transported from the tissue to liver is utilized for the resynthesize the of glucose and glycogen through Cori cycle Mayer Bodensky (1947) contributing to the increase in the level of lactic acid in liver and blood at all periods of study. Burton *et al.,* (1972) have observed the heavy accumulation of lactic acid in liver of rain brown trout *Salmo gairdneri* exposed to zinc. Qaisur and Shamim (2014) reported that impact of zinc sulphate on bio chemical parameter in *Channa gachua* reported that the decreased glycogen concentration in the liver could be due to its enhanced utilization as an immediate source to meet the energy demand under metallic stress through glycolysis or hexose monophosphate pathway. It is assumed that decrease in glycogen content may be due to the inhibition of hormones which contribute to glycogen synthesis. Depleted glycogen level under other heavy metals stress is also supports our findings with other workers. The increased in glucose level of tissue while decrement in tissue glycogen in exposed fish *Channa gachua* makes it clear that glycogen reserves are being used to meet the stress. To summarize these results indicate that the heavy metal at sub lethal and lethal concentrations are altered the bio chemical composition of the test fish due to utilization of biochemical energy to counteract the toxic stress due to heavy metals present in effluents.

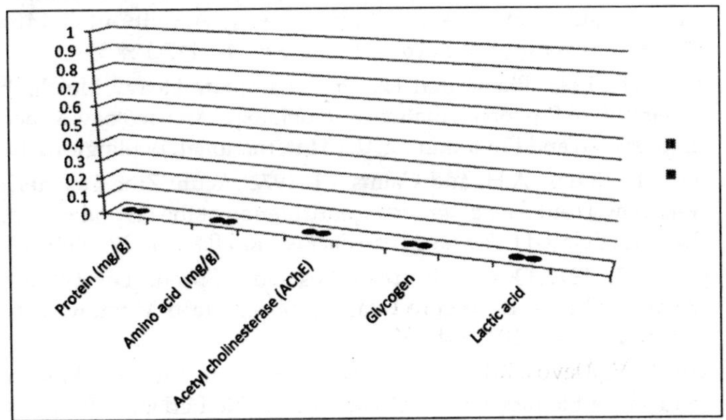

Graph 4.1: Showing biochemical parameters treated with Arsenic in *Channa gachua*

REFERENCES

Alam, M.G.M., Tanaka, A., Allinson, G., Laurenson, L.J.B., Stagnitti, F. and Snow, E.T.A. 2000. Comparison of Trace Element Concentrations in Cultured and Wild Carp (*Cyprinus carpio*) of Lake Kasumigaura. *Japan. Ecotoxicol. Environ.* 53: 348-354.

AlRmalli, S.W., Haris, P.I., Harrington, C.F., and Ayub, M.A. 2005. Survey of Arsenic in Food Stuffson Sale in the United Kingdom and Imported from Bangladesh. *Sci. Total. Environ.* 337: 23-30.

Ambika Shanmugam, 1980. Fundamentals of Biochemistry for Medical Students. Novabharat Offset Work pp. 350-411.

Anuradha, C.H., and Raju, T.N. 1996. Effect of Selenium Toxicity on Nuclei Acid, Protein and Free Amino Acid Contents of the Fish *Anabasscadens J. Ecotoxicol. Environ. Monit.* 6(3): 163-166.

Avasan Maruthi, Y., and Ramakrishna Rao, S. 2000. Effects of Sugar Mill Effluent on Organic Reserves of Fish. *Poll. Res.* 19(3): 391-393.

Barker S.B and Summerson, W.H. 1941. The Colorimetric Determination of Lactic Acid in Biological Material. *J. Biol. Chem.* 138: 535-554.

Bashamohideen, M. and Saibala, T. 1989. Acetylcholinesterase Activity in the Tissues of the Common Carp *Cypinus carpio* (Linnaeus) Subjected to the Sub Lethal Exposure of Malathion. *J. Environ. Biol.* 10(1): 51-57.

Baskaran, P., Palanichamy, S. and Arunachalam, S. 1989. Effects of Textile Dye Effluent of Feeding Energetic, Body Composition and Oxygen uptake of the Freshwater Fish *Oreochromismossambicus. J. Ecobiol.* 1: 203-214.

Bretaud, S.J., Toutant, P. and Saglio, P. 2000. Effects of Carbofuran diuron and nicosulfuron on Acetylcholine Sterase Activity in Goldfish (*Carassius auratus*) *Ecotoxicol. Environ. Safe.* 47: 117-124.

Brookes, R.R. 1998. Plants that Hyper Accumulate Heavy Metals, In: Their Role in Phytoremediation, Microbiology, Archaeology, Mineral Exploration and Phytomining, CAB International, Wallingford, UK.

Burton, T.D., Jones, A.H. and Caims, J.J. 1972. Acute Zinc Toxicity to Rainbow Trout *Salmo gairdneri* Confirmation of the Hypothesis that Death is Related to Tissue Hypoxia. *Fish. Res.Bd. Can.* 29: 1463-1466.

Coppage, D.L., 1972. Organophosphate Pesticides: Specific Level of Brain AchE Inhibition Related to Death in Sheep Head Minnow. *Trans. Ameri. Fish. Soc.* 101: 534-544.

Dokkun, W.V., Devos, R.H., Muys, T.H. and Wesstra, J.A. 1989. Minerals and Trace Elements in Total Diets in the Netherlands. *Br. J.Nutr.* 61: 7-15.

Elci, L.U. Divrikli, M. and Soylak, 2008. Inorganic Arsenic Speciation in Various Water Samples vith GF-AAS using Coprecipitation. *Int. J. Environ.Anal. Chem.* 88: 711-723.

Ghosh, T.K.,1990. Synthetic Pyrethroid Intoxication on Tissue Acetylcholine and acetylcholine Sterase in the Fish, *Tilapia mossambica. Environ. Ecol.* 8(3): 950-954.

Guo, H.R. 2002. Cancer Risk Assessment for Arsenic Exposure through Oyster Consumption. *Environ. Health Per.* 110:123-124.

Jana, S. and Bondyopadhyay, N.1981. Effects of Heavy Metals on some Biochemical Parameterin the Freshwater Fish, *Channa punctatus. Environ. Ecol.* 5(3): 488-493.

Jatyajit Hota, 1996. Arsenic Toxicity to the Brain, Liver and Intestine on a Freshwater Fish, *Channa punctatus* (Bloch). *J.Geobios.* 23:154- 156.

Jha, B.S and Jha, M.M. 1995. Biochemical Effects of Nickel Chloride on the Liver and Gonads of the Freshwater ClimbingPperch, *Anabastestudineus* (Bloch). *Proc. Nat. Acad. Sci. India.* 65(B): 39-46.

Karuppasamy, R. 2000. Short and Long Term Effects Phenyl Mercuric Acetate on Protein Metabolism in *Channa punctatus* (Bloch). *J. Natcon.* 12(1): 83-93.

Kaundinya, R.P. and Ramamurthy, R. 1978. Effect of Sumithion (Fentothion) on some Selected Enzyme System in the Fish, *Tilapiamossambica* (Peters). *Indian J. Exp. Biol.* 16: 809-811.

Kemp, A and Kitsven Hejhingeen, J.M. 1954. A Calorimetric Micro method for the Determination of Glycogen in Tissues. *Biochem. J.* 56: 640-648.

Lai, W.M.W. Cullen, S. Ray, 2001. Arsenic Speciation in Sea scallop gonads, Appl. Lake in Sindh (Pakistan), *J.Environ. Monit. Assess.* 141: 287-296.

Lowry, O.H., Rosenbrough, N.J., Farr, A. and Randall, R J. 1951. Proteins Measurement with Folinphenol Reagent. *J. Biol. Chem.* 193: 265-273.

Jakubis, M. and Nieuwenhuijsen, M.J. 2003. EXPASCAN Study Group, Association between Arsenic Exposure from a Coal-burning Power Plant and Urinary Arsenic Concentrations in Prievidza District, Slovakia. *Environ. Health Perspect.* 111: 89-894.

Malla Reddy, P. and Basha Mohideen M.D. 1988. Toxic Impact of Fenvalerate on the Protein Metabolism in the Branchial Tissue of a Fish *Cyprinus carpio. Curr. Sci.* 57: 211-212.

Manoharan, T. and Subbiah, G.N. 1982. Toxic Sublethal Effect of Endosulfan on *Barbus stigma. Proc. Indi. Acad. Sci. Anim. Sci.* 91(6): 523-532.

Mayer Bodensky. 1947. Introduction to Physical Chemistry. John Willey and Sons, New York. 314-462 pp.

McLeay, D.J. 1973. Effects of 12 Hour and 25 Days Exposure to Kraft Pulpmill Effluents on the Blood and Tissues of Juvenile Coho salmon (*Oncorhynchus kisutch*). *J.Fish. Res. Bd. Can.* 30: 395-400.

McLeay, D.J. and Brown, D.A. 1974. Growth and Stimulation and Biochemical Changes in Juvenile *Coho salmon* (*Oncorhynchus kisutch*) Exposed to Bleached Kraft Pulpmill Effluent for 200 days. *J.Fish. Res. Bd. Can.* 31: 1043-1049.

Meenakshi, V. and Indra, N. 1998. Sublethal Toxicity of Distillery Effluent on the Protein and Free Aminoacids of the Freshwater Fish, *Mystusvittatus* (Bloch). *J. Nat.Con.* 10(1): 87-91.

Metcalf, R.L. 1951. Methods in Biochemical Analysis. (Glick, D. Eds.) Vol. V. Interscience Publication. New York. 44 pp.

Metelev, V.V., Kanaev, A.I. and Dzasokhova, N.G. 1983. Water Toxicology. Amerind Publishing Co. Pvt. Ltd., New Delhi. pp. 56-60.

Nachmanson, D. and. Feld, F.A 1974. In: Insecticides Action and Metabolism (Ed., O' Brien R.D). Academic Press, Inc., New York.

Nath, B.S. and Kumar, R.P.S. 1999. Toxic Impact of Organo Phosphorous Insecticides on Acetylcholine Sterase Activity in the Silkworm, *Bombyxmori* L. *Ecotoxicol. Environ. Safe.* 42: 157-162.

Neff, J.M. 1985. Use of Biochemical Measurement to Defect Pollutant Mediated Damage to Fish. *ASTM. Spec. Tech. Publ.* 854: 155-183.

Nisha and Shukla, N.P.1986. Effect of Textile Liquid Effluent on the Freshwater Fish. *Indian J. Environ. Prot.* 69(3): 189-192.

Palanichamy, S., Arunachalam, S. and Baskaran, P. 1989. Impact of Pesticides on Protein Metabolism in the Freshwater Catfish, *Mystusvittatus. J. Ecobiol.* 1: 90-97.

Palanisamy, S. and Baskaran, P. 1995. Selected Biochemical and Physiological Response of the Fish *Channa striatus* as Biomonitor to Assess Heavy Metal Pollution in Freshwater Environment. *J. Ecotoxicol. Environ. Monit.* 5(2): 131-138.

Qaisur Rahman 2011. Studies on some Factors Affecting Aerial and Aquatic Respiration in an Air Breathing Fish *Channa gachua* (Ham.) Ph.D.Thesis, Vinoba Bhave University, Hazaribagh, Jharkhand, India.

Qaisur Rahman and Sadhu. D.N. 2012. Factors Affecting Aerial and Aquatic Respiration in the Air Breathing Fish *Channa gachua. J. Ecotoxicol. Environ. Monit.* 22(1): 17-30.

Qaisur Rahmanand Choudhary S. A. 2014. Impact of Zinc Sulphate on Biochemical Parameter in Reproductive Cycle in an Air Breathing Fish *Channa gachua. J. Himalayan. Ecol. Sustain. Dev.* 9: 74-80.

Rajamanickam, C. 1992. Effects of Heavy Metal Copper on the Biochemical Contents, Bio Accumulation and Histology of the Selected Organs in the Freshwater Fish, *Mystus vittatus* (Bloch) Ph.D. Thesis, Annamalai University.

Ramalingam V., Vimaladevi, V., Narmadaraj, R. and Prabaharan, P. 2000. Effect of Lead on Hematological and Biochemical Changes in Freshwater Fish, *Cirrhina mrigala. Poll. Res.* 19(1): 81-84.

Ramasamy, M. 1987. Effect of Sevin on Blood Free Amino Acids Level of the Fish *Sarotherodon mossambicus. Environ. Ecol.* 5: 633-637.

Rashed, M.N. 2001. Monitoring of Environmental Heavy Metals in Fish from Nasser Lake. *Environ. Int.* 27: 27-33.

Sankar Samipillai, S. and Jagadeesan, G. 2006a. Protective Role of Taurine on Mercuric Chloride induced Neurotoxicity in Rats. *Poll. Res.* 25: 39-43.

Sen, G., Bhera, M.K. and Patel, P. 1992. Effect of Zinc on Haemato biochemical Parameters of *Channa punctatus. J. Ecotoxicol. Environ.Monit.* 2(2): 89-92.

Sevgiler,Y., Elif OzCan Oruc, and Nevin Uner 2004. Evaluation of Pesticide Etoxazole Toxicity in the liver of *Oreochromis niloticus. J.biochem. Physiol.* 78: 18-24.

Smith, W.O., Marra, J., Hiscock, M.R. and Barber, R.T. 2000. The Seasonal Cycle of Phytoplankton Biomass and Primary Productivity in the Ross Sea, Antarctica, Deep Sea Res. PII 47: 3119-3140.

Srivastava, A.K. and Singh, N.N. 1980. Observation of Hyperglycemia in the Murrel *Channa punctatus* after Acute Exposure to Methyl Parathion. *Comp. Physiol. Ecol.* 5:100-107.

Svobodovo, Z.O. Celechovska, T. Randak, J. and Machova, 2002. Content of Arsenic in Arket Ready Rainbow Trout (*Oncorhynchu mykiss*). *Acta. Vet. Brno.* 71: 361-367.

Tao, S.S., Bolger, P.M. and Gosh, G.G.D., 1999. Dietary Arsenic Intakes in the United States. FDA Total Diet Study, September 1991 to December 1996, Food. *Addit. Contam.* 16: 465-472.

Tariq, J.M., Jaffar, M. and Moazzam., 1991. Concentration Correlations between Majorcations and Heavy Metals in Fish from the Arabian Sea. *Mar. Pollut. Bull.* 22: 562-565.

Tuzen, M. 2003. Determination of Heavy Metals in Fish Samples of the Middle Black Sea (Turkey) by Graphite Furnace Atomic Absorption Spectrometry. *Food Chem.* 80:119-123.

Vijayram, K. and Vasugi, S.R. 1989. Sublethal Effects of Pulp and Paper Mill Effluents on the Biochemistry of a Freshwater Fish *Rasboradaniconius. Indian J. Environ. Hlth.* 31(1): 36-42.

Yang, W.D. Dettbarn, 1996. Disosoprophyl Phosphoro Fluoridate induced Cholinergic Hyperactivity and Lipid Peroxidation. *Toxicol. Appl. Pharmacol.* 138: 48-53.

Pages: 44-56

Renewable Resources and Environment
Edited by: Dr. Baby Tabassum
ISBN: 978-93-5056-893-4
Edition: 2018
Published by: Discovery Publishing House Pvt. Ltd., New Delhi (India)

Soil Degradation in India Caused by Fertilizers

Neetu Singh

ABSTRACT

A third of India's soil has been degraded and this could cost a shadow on the sustainability of agriculture in near future. Land degradation is posing a major threat of India's food and environmental security, resulting from the loss in biological or productive capacity of soil. According to estimates of the Indian council of agricultural research (2010) of the total geographical area of 328.73mha, about 120.40mha is effected by various levels of land degradation. Excessive use of chemical fertilizers, specially in the north-western parts of the country was the major reason for soil degradation. India ranked third in world of fertilizer production and second biggest consumer of fertilizers in the world next only to China. In India 57 large and 64 medium sized chemical fertilizers units are running. Indian industries produce various types of chemical fertilizers e.g. Urea, DAP, Complex fertilizers, Ammonium Sulphate (AS) and calcium Ammonium Nitrate (CAN). Fertilizers are chemical substances that are used to enrich soil with specific nutrients to help grow. The main elements provided by fertilizers are typically nitrogen, phosphorus and potassium, although some another elements like calcium and sulfur are also supplied by certain commercial

Dept. of Zoology, Ramabai Ambedkar Govt. Degree College, Gajraula (Amroha)

fertilizers. Any chemical fertilizers when applied to the soil, fertilizers break down into their constituent components and the root system of the plants absorb only a given level of nutrients at a time leaving the rest of the fertilizer to leach leaching of these fertilizers pollute waterways. Chemical fertilizers have a serious impact on overall productivity biodiversity environment and human health excessive use of Urea is mainly noticed in states having strong irrigation network like Punjab, Haryana, Western Uttar Pradesh and Andhra Pradesh. Urea can cause algal blooms to produce toxins and its presence in the runoff from the fertilizers land may delay a role in the increase of toxic blooms. The over use of chemical fertilizers can lead to soil acidification, Mineral depletion in soil, Soil Friability effect, Destruction of micro organism of soil etc.

It is important for us to be aware of the effects of fertilizers and to use them carefully. According to soil science experts fertilizers are unnecessary. Healthy plant growth is dependent on having the right helper organisms in the soil, which take the mineral material from the soil and convert it into a plant available form. Organic farming practices use naturally time tested techniques that naturally prevents soil depletion, destruction and does not use chemical fertilizers and other agricultural chemicals that pollute our soil, air and waterways.

Keywords: degradation, fertilizers, productivity, DAP, AS, CAN, algal bloom, organisms.

INTRODUCTION

India is a country of more than 1000 million people. It is the seventh largest nation in the world which has 328.7 million ha. geographical area. It has 141 Mha net area and current cropping intensity of 135% the gross cropped area in India is 190 Mha. With the introduction of modern high yielding varieties and development of irrigation facilities during 2000s, consumption of chemical fertilizer has increased markedly. Before describe the effect of fertilizers, it is essential to know about fertilizers, how they work, need to use, their types, etc.

How fertilizers work: Fertilizers are chemical substances that are used to enrich soils with specific nutrients to help plants grow. The elements provided by fertilizers are typically nitrogen, phosphorus, and potassium, although other elements such as calcium and sulfur are also available within certain commercial fertilizers. When applied to the soil, fertilizers break down into these constituent components and are then absorbed through the root system of plants as a form of nourishment.

NEED TO USE

Mineral Deficiency in Agriculture Soil

Soil fertility is depend on its nutrient status means the amount and rates of nutrient supply for plant growth. An adequate supply of nutrients in soil is must for plants to grow well and produce high yields. It can be adversely effected by the shortage of even any one of the nutrient is needed.

Law of Minimum

Acc. to law of minimum every nutrient is unique. Means one nutrient cannot be substituted for another. Balanced nutrition is important in obtaining maximum yields. The most usual limitations concern nitrogen, phosphorus and potassium, followed by sulfur.

Nutrients are depleted with each Harvest

A closed nutrient cycle exists in undisturbed nature. Plants use soil nutrients for their growth and release them back during their life cycle. By this way amount of soil nutrients remain maintain in this cycle. This cycle is broken down due to our agriculture practices. Nutrients are taken out of the soil together with plants during each harvest. This loss is partially offset by the decomposition of organic matter in the soil minerals. But, this natural process is far too slow. Without an external input, the capacity of the soil to supply plants with nutrients is progressively reduced with every harvest.

To Feed World's Population

The FAO stated that "after land and water, fertilizers are probably the most important input leading yields". In the 'developed world', after 150 years of increasing fertilizer use, it is thought that roughly half of the present agricultural output may be attributed to fertilizers. It has been estimated that mineral fertilizers contribute about 40% of the nitrogen taken up by the world's crops.

So, on the basis of above reasons we can say that fertilizers are necessary to replace the nutrients that have been removed from the soil. They can provide an optimal nutrient balance, tailored to the demand of the specific crop, soil and climate conditions, increasing crop yield and quality.

List of common agricultural fertilizers:

- **Urea:** It is widely used granular type of solid nitrogen fertilizer. When applied to soil, urea reacts with water to form ammonia, which makes the nitrogen within the fertilizer available to plants. Urea delivers 46% amount of nitrogen, without phosphorus or potassium.
- **Ammonium Nitrate:** It is applied in granular form and provides substantial amounts of nitrogen to the soil. Ammonium nitrate typically provides 33% nitrogen.
- **Ammonium Sulfate:** It is a by-product, which is derived when sulfuric acid is used to remove ammonia from the coal used to make coke. It is a solid material that contains 21% nitrogen.
- **Calcium Nitrate:** It is less effective than other nitrogen fertilizers due to leaching when applied to soil. It is used to provide a readily source of nitrogen. It is also provide soluble calcium for soils that are calcium deficient.
- **Diammonium Phosphate:** It is applied in liquid form because of highly water soluble nature. It provides enough phosphate for soils which require. It is a major source of phosphate component, at around 46% and 18% of nitrogen.
- **Monoammonium Phosphate:** It is one another source of phosphorus. It has 48% phosphate component and 11% of nitrogen.

- **Triple Super phosphate:** It is a granular fertilizer and directly applied to the soil. It can be used commercially as well as in home applications. It is often combined with nitrogen-based fertilizers to provide a better, broad-spectrum application.
- **Potassium Nitrate:** It is commonly known as nitrate of potash and used on vegetable crops. It provides 44% of potassium component.
- **Potassium Chloride:** It can be direc.ly applied to soils or in liquid fertilizers. It can be combined into multiple endings of mixed fertilizers. This fertilizer provides 60 to 62% of potassium component.

India ranked third in World of fertilizer production and second biggest consumer of fertilizer in the world next only to China. In India 57 large sized and 64 medium and small sized chemical fertilizer production units are running. Indian industries produce various types of fertilizers as discuss above. Modern fertilizer consists of varying amounts of nitrogen (N), phosphorus (P) and potassium (K). These three are believed to be essential for plants to grow and are extracted from the soil with each harvest. Then why we are talking about the negative effects of fertilizers? These are so much helpful, i.e. why farmers spread fertilizers on their fields and get rich crop, what's wrong with it. It is all correct but here is one another side of this coin is also present which is very horrible.

R.B. Singh, Chancellor of Central Agricultural Uni., cautioned that by 2050, the world would have 9.6 billion people and most of the 'bulge' would come from India, China and South Asia. Can we feed such a large population that will need 60% more food? The answer lie in the quality of our soil, he said. Why he emphasize the term Quality of soil? Because, excessive use of fertilizers degrade our soil. Plants have the capacity to absorb only a given level of nutrients at a time leaving the rest of the fertilizer to leach. Leaching of these fertilizers pollute waterways. Chemical fertilizers have a serious impact on overall productivity, biodiversity, environment and human health.

SOIL DEGRADATION

Soil degradation can be defined as a process by which one or more of the potential ecological functions of the soil are harmed. This process lowers the current and/or future capacity of the soil to produce goods and services.

Soil Degradation Scenario of India

According to estimates of the Indian Council of Agricultural Research (2010-11), of the total geographical area of 328.73 mha, about 120.40 mha is affected by various levels of soil degradation. Excessive use of chemical fertilizers, especially in the north-western parts of the country, was one of the major reasons for soil degradation. Soil degradation is a serious threat and this could cost a shadow on the sustainability of agriculture in near future which will directly affect the food and environmental security of India.

HARMFUL EFFECTS OF CHEMICAL FERTILIZERS

Soil Acidification

The overuse of chemical fertilizers can lead to soil acidification due to decreasing of organic matter in the soil. Application of too much nitrogen in fields over time damages top soil, resulting in reduced crop yields. Sandy soils are much more prone to soil acidification than clay soils. Clay soils have an ability to buffer the effect of excess chemical fertilization.

Mineral Depletion

Application of chemical fertilizers on the same soil for a long time causes remarkable depletion of essential soil nutrients. So the quality of crop effects and the food produced in these soils have less vitamins and mineral content.

Ground Water Pollution

Plants have the capacity to absorb only a given level of nutrition at a time leaving the rest of the fertilizer to leach. Leaching is not only hazardous to ground water sources but also to the health of subsoil where these chemicals react with clay known as hardpan. In soil science hardpan or ouklip is a dense layer of soil, usually found below the uppermost topsoil layer. Hardpans restrict root growth and make it difficult for water, air, other gases plus soil organisms to move through the soil.

Soil Friability Effect

The presence of a number of acids in the soil, such as hydrochloric and sulfuric acids, create a damaging effect on soil referred to as soil friability. The different acids in the soil dissolve the soil crumbs which help to hold together the rock particles. Soil crumbs result from the combination of humus, or decomposed natural material such as dead leaves with clay. These mineral rich soil crumbs are essential to soil drainage and greatly improve air circulation in the soil. As the chemicals in the chemical fertilizers destroy soil crumbs, the result is a high compacted soil with reduced drainage and air circulation.

Destruction of Micro-Organisms

The synthetic chemicals in the chemical fertilizers adversely affect the health of naturally found soil micro-organisms by affecting the soil pH. These altered levels of acidity in the soil eliminate the micro-organisms beneficial to plant and soil health as they help to increase the plants natural defenses against pests and diseases. These helpful microorganisms consist of antibiotic producing bacteria and mycorrhizal and other fungi which are found in healthy soil.

Increased Micro-organisms

Nitrogen rich chemical fertilizers can have the complete opposite effect on soil in comparison to more acidic fertilizers. Too much nitrogen can lead to a microorganism population boom. In large enough numbers, these microorganisms, instead of helping plants, will hurt them, as they will consume all of the organic material and nutrients in the surrounding soil.

Looming Shortage of Nutrients

Unfortunately, the Earth's soil is now being depleted of nutrients at more than 13% the rate it can be replaced. Not only that, but acc. to some, we also be facing looming shortage of two critical fertilizer ingredients: phosphorus and potassium. According to Jeremy Grantham, writing for nature: "These two elements cannot be made, cannot be substituted, are necessary to grow all life forms, and are mind and depleted. It's a scary set of statements. Former Soviet states and Canada have more than 70% of the potash. Morocco has 85% of all high-grade phosphates. It is the most important quasi-monopoly in economic history. What happen when these fertilizers run out? There seems to be only one conclusion: their use must be drastically reduced in the next 20-40 years or we will begin to starve."

Table 5.1

Severity of soil degradation (Slight, 5-10 tonnes; moderate, 11-20 tonnes; high 21-40 tonnes and severe, more than 40 tonnes)

Degradation	Severity of Degradation				Total Area (Million ha)
	Slight	Moderate	High	Severe	
Water erosion	5.0	24.3	107.2	12.7	148.9
Wind erosion	0.0	0.0	10.8	2.7	13.5
Loss of nutrients	0.0	0.0	3.7	0.0	3.7
Salinization	2.8	2.0	5.3	0.0	10.1
Water-logging	6.4	5.2	0.0	0.0	11.6
Total	14.2	31.5	127.0	15.1	187.7

Other Effects

In particular, above optimum nitrogen and phosphorus levels can lead to excessive plant and algal growth in waterways that can degrade drinking water, fisheries and recreational areas. High potassium can lead to an imbalance of base saturation levels as well as high soluble salts. High calcium and magnesium levels are commonly associated with pH values above 7.0. Urea can cause algal blooms to produce toxins, and its presence in the runoff from fertilizers land may play a role in the increase of toxic blooms. Acc. to a geographical article; "Runaway nitrogen is suffocating wildlife in lakes and estuaries, contaminating groundwater, and even warming the globe's climate.

Nitrogen is both an essential nutrient and a major pollutant in terrestrial ecosystems. As an integral component of essential plant nutrients, nitrogen plays an important role in increasing crop quality. 78% of gaseous nitrogen (N2), appears to a virtually limitless reservoir the two nitrogen atoms make this gas quite inert and not directly usable by plants and animals. Introducing of reactive nitrogen such as nitrate ($NO3^{-}$), ammonium ($NH4^{+}$), or urea, which rapidly hydrogen to form $NH4^{+,}$ to the terrestrial biosphere, that is, fertilization, has been recognized as the most effective method for increasing food production. However excess nitrogen used in fertilization has undoubtedly disturbed the biogeochemical nitrogen cycle of natural ecosystem, resulting in various global, regional and local environmental problems such as stratospheric ozone depletion, soil acidification and especially $NO3^-$, pollution of ground surface water.

In contrast to $NH4^+$ ions, $NO3^-$ ions are not absorbed by the negatively charged colloids that dominant most soils. Therefore, $NO3^-$ ions move downward freely with drainage water and are thus readily leached from the soil. Such leaching losses not only cause several serious environmental problems, but also reduce ecosystem productivity.

Prevention, Healing and Conservation of Soil from Degradation

It is important for us to be aware about the effect of fertilizers and use them carefully.

Crop Cycle

Mono cropping is the high-yield agriculture practice of growing a single crop year after year on the same land, in the absence of rotation through other crops. Corn, soybeans, wheat, and to some degree rice, are the most common crops grown with mono cropping techniques.

By contrast, poly cropping (the traditional rotation of crops and livestock) better serves both land and people. Poly cropping evolved to meet the complete nutritional needs of a local community. Poly cropping, when done mindfully, automatically replenishes what is taken out, which makes it sustainable with minimal effort.

Improve Right helper Organisms

A key component of successful agriculture lies in having the right helper organisms in the soil; beneficial species of bacteria, fungi, protozoa, beneficial nematodes (not the weed feeders), micro arthropods and earthworms.

According to soil science expert, fertilizers are unnecessary. Healthy plant growth is dependent on having the right helper organisms in the soil, which take the mineral material from the soil and convert it into a plant-available form. Without these bio-organisms, plants cannot get the nutrients they need. They supply to plant with precisely the right balances of all the nutrients the plant requires.

Green Manure

In agriculture, green manure is created by leaving uprooted or sown crop parts to wither on a field so that they serve as a mulch and soil amendment. The plants used for green manure are often cover crops grown primarily for this purpose. Typically, they are ploughed under and incorporated into the soil while green or shortly after flowering. Green manure is commonly associated with organic farming and can play an important role in sustainable annual cropping systems. Green manure performs the vital function of fertilization. It acts mainly as soil-acidifying matter to decrease the alkalinity/pH of alkali soils.

Use of Biomass

Biomass is organic matter derived from living, or recently living organisms. The increased percentage of biomass improves water infiltration and retention, aeration, and other soil characteristics.

Cover Crop

Cover crops such as legumes, white turnip, radishes and other species are rotated with cash crops to blanket the soil year-round. Incorporation of cover crops into the soil allows the nutrients held within the green manure to be released and made available to the succeeding crops. This results immediately from an increase in abundance of soil microorganisms from the degradation of plant material that aid in the decomposition of this fresh material. This additional decomposition also allows for the reincorporation of nutrients that are found in the soil in a particular form such as nitrogen (N), potassium (K), phosphorus (P), calcium (Ca), magnesium

(Mg), and sulfur (S). Common cover crop functions of weed suppression. Some green crops reduced plant insect pests and diseases.

Strip Cropping

It consist of growing erosion permitted crop (e.g. Jowar, Bajra, Maize etc.) in alternate strips with erosion checking close growing crops (e.g. grasses, pulses etc.). strip cropping employs several good farming practices including crop rotation, contour cultivation, proper tillage, stubbles mulching, cover cropping etc.

Not only all above, but organic farming practices use natural, time-tested techniques that naturally prevents soil depletion and destruction, and doesn't use chemical fertilizers and other agricultural chemicals that pollute our soil, air, and waterways.

Govt. policies also influence all above mention measures. There is separate Department of Agriculture and cooperation in Ministry of Agriculture of Govt. of India. This dep. Conduct various types of programmes for degraded land development and collect data of achievements and there impacts on soil degradation. Govt. of India move to provide 'Soil Health Cards' to all farmers across the country in next three year may help them take judicious decision based on nutrient related information for different soil types."

It's not the end but a starting point towards healthy soil. "Take care of soil and the soil will take care of the plants."

REFERENCES

Annual Report Pb (2012) Annual Report from Punjab Environmental Centre.

FAI (2010) FAO Fertilizer Statistics 2005-06. Fertilizer Association of India, New Delhi.

Govt. of India, Ministry of Agriculture, Department of Agriculture & Cooperation, New Delhi.

Gupta, A.P. (2005) Nitrogen Use Scenario of India. Science in China Ser. C Life Sciences, 48, 921-927.

Iasrai (2006) Agricultural Research Data Book. Indian Agricultural Statistics Research Institute, New Delhi.

Prasad, R. (2006) Efficient Fertilizer Use: The Key to Food Security and Better Environment. Journal of Tropical Agriculture, 47, 1-17.

Pages: 57-71

Renewable Resources and Environment

Edited by: Dr. Baby Tabassum

ISBN: 978-93-5056-893-4

***Edition:* 2018**

***Published by:* Discovery Publishing House Pvt. Ltd., New Delhi (India)**

Environmental Problems and Sustainable Development

With Special Reference to India Issues and Challenge

Kalpana Singh and Shikha Yadav

There are many environmental issues in India. Air pollution, water pollution, garbage, and pollution of the natural environment are all challenges for India. The situation was worse between 1947 through 1995. According to data collection and environment assessment studies of World Bank experts, between 1995 through 2010, India has made one of the fastest progresses in the world, in addressing its environmental issues and improving its environmental quality. Still, India has a long way to go to reach environmental quality similar to those enjoyed in developed economies. Pollution remains a major challenge and opportunity for India. Environmental issues are one of the primary causes of disease, health issues and long term livelihood impact for India.

HISTORY

Asoka Pillar Edicts were one of earliest efforts in India that focused on respecting and preserving environment, forests and wildlife. Yajnavalkya Smite, a historic Indian text on statecraft and jurisprudence, suggested to have been written before the 5th century AD, prohibited the cutting of trees and prescribed punishment for such acts. Antalya's Arthashastra, written in Maryann period, emphasized the

Dept. of Zoology & Chemistry, R.S. Govt. College Shivrajpur, Kanpur (U.P.) (India)

need for forest administration. Asoka went further, and his Pillar Edicts expressed his view about the welfare of environment and biodiversity. "Happiness in this world and the next is difficult to obtain without much love for the dharma, much self-examination, much respect, much fear of evil, and much enthusiasm. [...] Beloved-of-the-Gods, King Piyadasi (Asoka), speaks thus: Animals were declared to be protected – parrots, manias, arena, geese, wild ducks, nandimukhas, gelatos, bats, queen ants, terrapins, boneless fish, vedareyaka, gangapuputaka, snaky fish, tortoises, porcupines, squirrels, deer, bulls, ocarina, wild asses, wild pigeons, domestic pigeons and all four-footed creatures that are neither useful nor edible. Also protected were nanny goats, ewes and sows which are with young or giving milk to their young, and so are young ones less than six months old. Cocks are not to be caponized, husks hiding living beings are not to be burnt, and forests are not to be burnt either without reason or to kill creatures. One animal is not to be fed to another. Our king killed very few animals."

ASHOKA'S SEVEN PILLAR EDICTS

British rule of India saw several laws related to environment. Amongst the earliest ones were Shore Nuisance (Bombay and Koala) Act of 1853 and the Oriental Gas Company Act of 1857. The Indian Penal Code of 1860 imposed a fine on anyone who voluntarily fouls the water of any public spring or reservoir. In addition, the Code penalized negligent acts. British India also enacted laws aimed at controlling air pollution. Prominent amongst these were the Bengal Smoke Nuisance Act of 1905 and the Bombay Smoke Nuisance Act of 1912. Whilst these laws upon independence from Britain, India adopted a constitution and numerous British-enacted laws, without any specific constitutional provision on protecting the environment. India amended its constitution in 1976. Article 48(A) of Part IV of the amended constitution, read: The State shall Endeavour to protect and improve the environment and to safeguard the forests and wildlife of the country. Article 51 A (g) imposed additional environmental mandates on the Indian state. Other Indian laws from recent history include the Water (Prevention and Control of Pollution) Act of 1974, the Forest (Conservation) Act of 1980, and the Air (Prevention and Control of Pollution) Act of 1981. The Air Act was inspired by the decisions made at Stockholm Conference. The Bhopal gas tragedy triggered the Government of India to enact the Environment (Protection) Act of 1986. India has also enacted a set of Noise Pollution (Regulation & Control) Rules in 2000. In 1985, Indian government created the Ministry of Environment and Forests. This ministry is the central administrative organization in India for regulating and ensuring environmental protection. Despite active passage of laws by the central government of India, the reality of environmental quality mostly worsened between 1947 to 1990. Most of Indian economy was nationalized and owned by India, and regulations were mostly ignored by state run enterprises. Rural poor had no choice, but to sustain life in whatever way possible. The state governments of India often regarded environmental laws enacted by the central government as a mere paperwork formality. Air emissions increased, water pollution worsened, forest cover decreased. Starting in the 1990s, reforms were introduced. Since then, for the first time in Indian history, major air pollutant concentrations have dropped in every 5-year period. Between 1992 to 2010, satellite data confirms India's forest coverage has increased for the first time by over 4 million hectares, a 7% increase.

OBJECTIVES OF THE STUDY

1. To describe and discuss the common characteristics of health system functioning in the given socioeconomic, socio-cultural, political and ecological settings.
2. To highlight and delineate crucial factors responsible for the health sector reforms and to undertake, as the most challenging endeavor, effective and efficient health management and equality health care service provisions in the community.

3. The fundamental objective is to act as a catalyst in bringing about local initiative and community participation in overall improvement in quality of life.

CAUSES

Some have cited economic development as the cause regarding the environmental issues. Others believe economic development is key to improving India's environmental management and preventing pollution of the country. It is also suggested that India's growing population is the primary cause of India's environmental degradation. Systematic studies challenge this theory. Empirical evidence from countries such as Japan, England and Singapore, each with population density similar or higher than India, yet each enjoying environmental quality vastly superior to India, suggests population density may not be the only factor affecting India.

MAJOR ENVIRONMENTAL ISSUES

Major environmental issues are forest and agricultural degradation of land, resource depletion (water, mineral, forest, sand, rocks etc.), environmental degradation, public health, loss of biodiversity, loss of resilience ecosystems, and livelihood security for the poor. The major sources of pollution in India include the rampant burning of fuel wood and biomass such as dried waste from livestock as the primary source of energy, lack of organized garbage and waste removal services, lack of sewage treatment operations, lack of flood control and monsoon water drainage system, diversion of consumer waste into rivers, cremation practices near major rivers, government mandated protection of highly polluting old public transport, and continued operation by Indian government of government owned, high emission plants built between 1950 to 1980. Air pollution, poor management of waste, growing water scarcity, falling groundwater tables, water pollution, preservation and quality of forests, biodiversity loss, and land/soil degradation are some of the major environmental issues India faces today. India's population growth adds pressure to environmental issues and its resources.

POPULATION GROWTH AND ENVIRONMENTAL QUALITY

There is a long history of study and debate about the interactions between population growth and the environment. According to a British thinker Malthus, for example, a growing population exerts pressure on agricultural land, causing environmental degradation, and forcing the cultivation of land of poorer as well as poorer quality. This environmental degradation ultimately reduces agricultural yields and food availability, causes famines and diseases and death, thereby reducing the rate of population growth. Population growth, because it can place increased pressure on the assimilative capacity of the environment, is also seen as a major cause of air, water, and solid-waste pollution. The result, Malthus theorized, is an equilibrium population that enjoys low levels of both income and environmental quality. Malthus suggested positive and preventative forced control of human population, along with abolition of poor laws. Malthus theory, published between 1798 and 1826, has been analyzed and criticized ever since. The American thinker Henry George, for example, observed with his characteristic piquancy in dismissing Malthus: "Both the jay hawk and the man eat chickens; but the more Jayhawks, the fewer chickens, while the more men, the more chickens." Similarly, the American economist Julian Lincoln Simon criticized Malthus's theory. He noted that the facts of human history have proven the predictions of Malthus and of the Neo-Malthusians to be flawed. Massive geometric population growth in the 20th century did not result in a Malthusian catastrophe. The possible reasons include: increase in human knowledge, rapid increases in productivity, innovation and application of knowledge, general improvements in farming methods (industrial agriculture), mechanization of work (tractors), the introduction of high-yield varieties of wheat and other plants (Green Revolution), and the use of pesticides to control crop pests. India's population density, in 2011, was about 368 human beings per square kilometer. Many countries with population density similar or higher than India enjoy environmental quality as well as human quality of life far superior than India. For example: Singapore (7148/km^2), Hong Kong (6349/km^2), South Korea (487/km^2), Netherlands (403/km^2), Belgium (355/km^2), England (395/km^2) and Japan (337/km^2).

WATER POLLUTION

India has major water pollution issues. Discharge of untreated sewage is the single most important cause for pollution of surface and ground water in India. There is a large gap between generation and treatment of domestic waste water in India. The problem is not only that India lacks sufficient treatment capacity but also that the sewage treatment plants that exist do not operate and are not maintained. The majority of the government-owned sewage treatment plants remain closed most of the time due to improper design or poor maintenance or lack of reliable electricity supply to operate the plants, together with absentee employees and poor management. The waste water generated in these areas normally percolates in the soil or evaporates. The uncollected wastes accumulate in the urban areas cause unhygienic conditions and release pollutants that leach to surface and groundwater. According to a World Health Organization study, out of India's 3,119 towns and cities, just 209 have partial sewage treatment facilities, and only 8 have full wastewater treatment facilities. Over 100 Indian cities dump untreated sewage directly into the Ganges River. Investment is needed to bridge the gap between 29000 million liter per day of sewage India generates, and a treatment capacity of mere 6000 million liter per day. Other sources of water pollution include agriculture run off and small scale factories along the rivers and lakes of India. Fertilizers and pesticides used in agriculture in northwest have been found in rivers, lakes and ground water. Flooding during monsoons worsens India's water pollution problem, as it washes and moves all sorts of solid garbage and contaminated soils into its rivers and wetlands.

WATER RESOURCES

According to NASA groundwater declines are highest on Earth between 2002 and 2008 in northern India. Agricultural productivity is dependent on irrigation. A collapse of agricultural output and severe shortages of potable water may influence 114 million residents in India. In July 2012, about 670 million people or 10% of the world's population lost power blame on the severe drought restricting the power delivered by hydroelectric dams. A rural stove using biomass cakes, fuel wood and trash as cooking fuel. Surveys suggest over 100 million households in India use such stoves (chullahs) every day, 2-3 times a day. It is a major source of air pollution in India, and produces smoke and numerous indoor air pollutants at concentrations 5 times higher than coal. Clean burning fuels and electricity are unavailable in rural parts and small towns of India because of poor rural highways and limited energy generation infrastructure. Air pollution in India is a serious issue with the major sources being fuel wood and biomass burning, fuel adulteration, vehicle emission and traffic congestion. Air pollution is also the main cause of the Asian brown cloud, which is causing the monsoon to be delayed. India is the world's largest consumer of fuel wood, agricultural waste and biomass for energy purposes. Traditional fuel (fuel wood, crop residue and dung cake) dominates domestic energy use in rural India and accounts for about 90% of the total. In urban areas, this traditional fuel constitutes about 24% of the total. Fuel wood, agric waste and biomass cake burning releases over 165 million tones of combustion products into India's indoor and outdoor air every year. These biomass-based household stoves in India are also a leading source of greenhouse emissions contributing to climate change. The annual crop burning practice in northwest India, north India and eastern Pakistan, after monsoons, from October to December, are a major seasonal source of air pollution. Approximately 500 million tons of crop residues is burnt in open, releasing smoke, soot, Knox, Sox, PAHs and particulate matter into the air. This burning has been found to be a leading cause of smog and haze problems through the winter over Punjab, cities such as Delhi, and major population centers along the rivers through West Bengal. In other states of India, rice straw and other crop residue burning in open is a major source of air pollution. Vehicle emissions are another source of air pollution. Vehicle emissions are worsened by fuel adulteration and poor fuel combustion efficiencies from traffic congestion and low density of quality, high speed road network per 1000 people. On per capita basis, India is a small emitter of carbon dioxide greenhouse. In 2009, IEA estimates that it emitted about 1.4 tons of gas per person, in comparison to the United States' 17 tons per person, and a world average of 5.3 tons per person. However, India was the third largest emitter of total carbon dioxide in 2009 at 1.65 Get per year, after China (6.9 Get per year) and the United States (5.2 Get per year). With 17 percent of world population, India contributed some 5 percent of human-sourced carbon dioxide emission; compared to China's 24 percent share. The Air (prevention and control of pollution) Act was passed in 1981 to regulate air pollution and there have been some measurable improvements. However, the 2012 Environmental Performance Index ranked India as having the poorest relative air quality out of 132 countries.

SOLID WASTE POLLUTION

Trash and garbage is a common sight in urban and rural areas of India. It is a major source of pollution. Indian cities alone generate more than 100 million tons of solid waste a year. Street corners are piled with trash. Public places and sidewalks are despoiled with filth and litter, rivers and canals act as garbage dumps. In part, India's garbage crisis is from rising consumption. India's waste problem also points to a stunning failure of governance. In 2000, India's Supreme Court directed all Indian cities to implement a comprehensive waste-management programmed that would include household collection of segregated waste, recycling and composting. These directions have simply been ignored. No major city runs a comprehensive programmed of the kind envisioned by the Supreme Court. Indeed, forget waste segregation and recycling directive of the India's Supreme Court, the Organization for Economic Cooperation and Development estimates that up to 40 percent of municipal waste in India remains simply uncollected. Even medical waste, theoretically controlled by stringent rules that require hospitals to operate incinerators, is routinely dumped with regular municipal garbage. A recent study found that about half of India's medical waste is improperly disposed of. Municipalities in Indian cities and towns have waste collection employees. However, these are unionized government workers and their work performance is neither measured nor monitored. Some of the few solid waste landfills India has, near its major cities, are overflowing and poorly managed. They have become significant sources of greenhouse emissions and breeding sites for disease vectors such as flies, mosquitoes, cockroaches, rats, and other pests.[38] In 2011, several Indian cities embarked on waste-to-energy projects of the type in use in Germany, Switzerland and Japan.[39] For example, New Delhi is implementing two incinerator projects aimed at turning the city's trash problem into electricity resource. These plants are being welcomed for addressing the city's chronic problems of excess untreated waste and a shortage of electric power. They are also being welcomed by those who seek to prevent water pollution, hygiene problems, and eliminate rotting trash that produces potent greenhouse gas methane. The projects are being opposed by waste collection workers and local unions who fear changing technology may deprive them of their livelihood and way of life. Along with waste-to-energy projects, some cities and towns such as Pane, Maharashtra are introducing competition and the privatization of solid waste collection, street cleaning operations and bio-mining to dispose the waste. A scientific study suggests public private partnership is, in Indian context, more useful in solid waste management. According to this study, government and municipal corporations must encourage PPP-based local management through collection, transport and segregation and disposal of solid waste.

NOISE POLLUTION

The supreme court of India which is in New Delhi gave a significant verdict on noise pollution in 2005. Unnecessary honking of vehicles makes for a high decibel level of noise in cities. The use of loudspeakers for political purposes and for sermons by temples and mosques makes noise pollution in residential areas worse. In January 2010, Government of India published norms of permissible noise levels in urban and rural areas.

LAND OR SOIL POLLUTION

In March 2009, the issue of Uranium Poisoning in Punjab attracted press coverage. It was alleged to be caused by fly ash ponds of thermal power stations, which reportedly lead to severe birth defects in children in the Faridkot and Bhatinda districts of Punjab. The news reports claimed the uranium levels were more than 60 times the maximum safe limit. In 2012, the Government of India confirmed that the ground water in Malawi belt of Punjab has uranium metal that is 50% above the trace limits set by the United Nations' World Health Organization. Scientific studies, based on over 1000 samples from various sampling points, could not trace the source to fly ash and any sources from thermal power plants or industry as originally alleged. The study also revealed that the uranium concentration in ground water of Malawi district is not 60 times the WHO limits, but only 50% above the WHO limit in 3 locations. This highest concentration found in samples was less than those found naturally in ground waters currently used for human purposes elsewhere, such as Finland. Research is underway to identify natural or other sources for the uranium.

ENVIRONMENTAL ISSUES AND INDIAN LAW

Since about the late 1980s, the Supreme Court of India has been pro-actively engaged in India's environmental issues. In most countries, it is the executive and the legislative branches of the government that plan, implement and address environmental issues; the Indian experience is different. The

Supreme Court of India has been engaged in interpreting and introducing new changes in the environmental jurisprudence directly. The Court has laid down new principles to protect the environment, re-interpreted environmental laws, created new institutions and structures, and conferred additional powers on the existing ones through a series of directions and judgments. The Court's directions on environmental issues go beyond the general questions of law, as is usually expected from the highest Court of a democratic country. The Supreme Court of India, in its order, includes executive actions and technical details of environmental actions to be implemented. Indeed, some critics of India's Supreme Court describe the Court as the Lords of Green Bench or Garbage Supervisor. Supporters of India's Supreme Court term these orders and the Indian bench as pioneering, both in terms of laying down new principles of law, and in delivering environmental justice. The reasons for the increasing interjection of India's Supreme Court in governance arenas are, experts claim, complex. A key factor has been the failure of government agencies and the state owned enterprises in discharging their Constitutional and Statutory duties. This has prompted civil society groups to file public interest complaints with the Courts, particularly the Supreme Court, for suitable remedies. Public interest litigation and judicial activism on environmental issues extends beyond India's Supreme Court. It includes the High Courts of individual states. India's judicial activism on environmental issues has, some suggest, delivered positive effects to the Indian experience. Proponents claim that the Supreme Court has, through intense judicial activism, become a symbol of hope for the people of India. As a result of judicial activism, India's Supreme Court has delivered a new normative regime of rights and insisted that the Indian state cannot act arbitrarily but must act reasonably and in public interest on pain of its action being invalidated by judicial intervention. Judicial activism in India has, in several key cases, found state-directed economic development ineffective and a failure, then interpreted laws and issued directives that encourage greater competition and free market to reduce environmental pollution. In other cases, the interpretations and directives have preserved industry protection, labor practices and highly polluting state-owned companies detrimental to environmental quality of India. Proactive measures should be taken to conserve the depleting environment.

FORESTS AND CONSERVATION

Ecological issues are an integral and important part of environmental issues challenging India. Poor air quality, water pollution and garbage pollution all affect the food and environment quality necessary for ecosystems. India is a large and diverse country. Its land area includes regions with some of the world's highest rainfall to very dry deserts, coast line to alpine regions, river deltas to tropical islands. The variety and distribution of forest vegetation is large. India is one of the 12 mega biodiversity regions of the world. Indian forests types include tropical evergreens, tropical deciduous, swamps, mangroves, sub-tropical, montage, scrub, sub-alpine and alpine forests. These forests support a variety of ecosystems with diverse flora and fauna. Until recently, India lacked an objective way to determine the quantity of forests it had, and the quality of forests it had.

These laws did not have the effect they intended:

In 1985, India created the Ministry of Environment and Forests. This was followed by a National Forest Policy and the major government reforms of the early 1990s. Over the last 20 years, India has reversed the deforestation trend. Specialists of the United Nations report India's forest as well as woodland cover has increased. A 2010 study by the Food and Agriculture Organization ranks India amongst the 10 countries with the largest forest area coverage in the world (the other nine being Russian Federation, Brazil, Canada, United States of America, China, Democratic Republic of the Congo, Australia, Indonesia and Sudan).[4] India is also one of the top 10 countries with the largest primary forest coverage in the world, according to this study. From 1990 to 2000, FAO finds India was the fifth largest gainer in forest coverage in the world; whilst from 2000 to 2010, FAO considers India as the third largest gainer in forest coverage.

National Forest Commission and India's a Forestation Programme In 2003, India set up a National Forest Commission to review and assess India's policy and law, its effect on India's forests, its impact of local forest communities, and to make recommendations to achieve sustainable forest and ecological security in India.[57] The report made over 300 recommendations including the following:

India must pursue rural development and animal husbandry policies to address local communities need to find affordable cattle fodder and grazing. To avoid destruction of local forest cover, fodder must reach these communities on reliable roads and other infrastructure, in all seasons year round.

The Forest Rights Bill is likely to be harmful to forest conservation and ecological security. The Forest Rights Bill became a law since 2007.

The government should work closely with mining companies. Revenue generated from lease of mines must be pooled into a dedicated fund to conserve and improve the quality of forests in the region where the mines are located.

Power to declare ecologically sensitive areas must be with each Indian state.

The mandate of State Forest Corporations and government owned monopolies must be changed.

Government should reform regulations and laws that ban felling of trees and transit of wood within India. Sustainable agro-forestry and farm forestry must be encouraged through financial and regulatory reforms, particularly on privately owned lands.

What we can do for the protection of environment:

1. Educate the students about the pollution problem and the harmful effects of pollution.

2. We should minimize the use plastic cover for different purposes.
3. Buy only environment friendly products i.e. the products which are not reducing the natural resources.
4. Not to waste water for various purposes.
5. To plant and grow trees in the house garden.
6. To motivate research on different measures to be taken to solve environmental problems.
7. To support the initiates taken by the central and state government in protecting our environment.

REFERENCES

Antony Reweaves: "Malthus Foiled again and again", in Nature 418, 668-670 (8 August 2002), Retrieved 28 December 2008.

Atman and *et al*. (2009). "Energy and Sustainable Development–An Indian Perspective"(PDF). World Academy of Science.

"Buddha Nullah the Toxic vein of Malawi". Indian Express. May 21, 2008.

David Pennies and Kirk Smith. "Biomass Pollution Basics" (PDF). The World Health Organization.

Decade of Drought: A Global Tour of Seven Recent Water Crises Guardian 12.6.2015.

"Drowning in a Sea of Garbage". The New York Times. 22 April 2010.

"Environmental Assessment, Country Data: India". The World Bank. 2011.

Environmental Issues, Law and Technology – An Indian Perspective. Ramesha Chandrappa and Ravi. D.R, Research India Publication, Delhi, 2009, ISBN 978-81-904362-5-0

"Evaluation of Operation and Maintenance of Sewage Treatment Plants in India- 2007" (PDF). Central Pollution Control Board, Ministry of Environment & Forests. 2008.

Ganguly *et al*. (2001). "Indoor Air Pollution In India – A Major Environmental and Public Health Concern" (PDF). Indian Council of Medical Research, New Delhi.

"Global Forest Resources Assessment 2010" (PDF). FAO. 2011.

Henrik Udall (July 2005). "People vs. Malthus: Population Pressure, Environmental Degradation, and Armed Conflict Revisited". Journal of Peace Research 42 (4): 417-434. doi:10.1177/0022343305054089.

"India: Country Strategy Paper, 2007-2013" (PDF). European External Action Service, European Union. 2007.

Klement Tockner and Jack A. Stanford (2002). "Reverie Flood Plains: Present State and Future Trends". Environmental Conservation 29 (3): 308-330.doi: 10.1017/S037689290200022X.

Maureen Cropper; Charles Griffiths (May 1994). "The Interaction of Population Growth and Environmental Quality" (PDF). The American Economic Review 84 (2): 250-254.

Milind Kandlikar, Gurumurthy Ramachandran (2000). "2000: India: The Causes and Consequences of Particulate Air Pollution in Urban India: A Synthesis of the Science". Annual Review of Energy and the Environment 25: 629-684.doi:10.1146/annurev.energy.25.1.629.

National Geographic Society. 1995. Water: A Story of Hope. Washington (DC): National Geographic Society.

Selden Thomas M. and Song Daqing (1994). "Environmental Quality and Development: Is There a Kuznets Curve for Air Pollution Emissions?" (PDF). Journal of Environmental Economics and Management 27 (2): 147-162. doi:10.1006/jeem.1994.1031.

Simon J.L. 1981. The Ultimate Resource; and 1992 the Ultimate Resource II.

"Status of Sewage Treatment in India" (PDF). Central Pollution Control Board, Ministry of Environment & Forests, Govt of India. 2005.

Steve Hamnera; Tripathi, Anshuman; Mishra, Rajesh Kumar; Bouskill, Nik; Broadaway, Susan C.; Pyle, Barry H.; Ford, Timothy E. *et al.* (2006). "The Role of Water use Patterns and Sewage Pollution in Incidence of Water-borne/Enteric Diseases along the Ganges River in Varanasi, India". International Journal of Environmental Health Research 16 (2): 113-32. Doi: 10.1080/09603120500538226. PMID 16546805.

Sushil and Batra; Batra, V (December 2006). "Analysis of Fly Ash Heavy Metal Content and Disposal in Three Thermal Power Plants in India". Fuel 85 (17-18): 2676-2679. doi:10.1016/j.fuel.2006.04.031.

"The Little Green Data Book". The World Bank. 2010.

"The Edicts of King Asoka (also, see other translations)". Buddhist Publication Society. 1994.

World Health Organization (1992), Our Planet, our Health: Report of the WHO Commission on Health and Environment, Geneva.

Pages: 72-80

Renewable Resources and Environment
Edited by: Dr. Baby Tabassum
ISBN: 978-93-5056-893-4
Edition: 2018
Published by: Discovery Publishing House Pvt. Ltd., New Delhi (India)

Protective Role of *Brassica Compestris* on Cadmium Toxicity in *Channa Punctatus*

Nida Idrees; Baby Tabassum
Priya Bajaj and Robeena Sarah

ABSTRACT

In present scenario of globalization, countries become more industrialized and want to become more powerful and developed. In this competitive era, industries like electrical, mining, dyes, chemical industries are emerged as a big source of income in a country as well as a major culprit of pollution. Heavy metal pollution is the major pollutant of present day concern. Most common heavy metals like lead (Pb), mercury (Hg), cadmium (Cd) and arsenic (As) are toxic to human health. Industries like electrical (inverter-batteries and stabilizers), mining, dyes, chemical industries are the major culprits of Cadmium toxicity. Due to these industries effluents, heavy metals deposit slowly in the surrounding water and in soil and get incorporated into food chain and disturb the biochemical process. *Channa punctatus* is edible fresh water fish may hold the cadmium concentration which indirectly reached in human body. When it occurred in the living body causes deformalities, diseases and even death. They are continuously affecting flora and fauna. The matter of concern is due to disturbing the ecological balance at every aspect. Concentration of cadmium is increasing in the form of

Department of Zoology, Govt. Raza P.G. College Rampur (U.P.) (India)
email: nidaidrees999@gmail.com

electronic and electrical Wastes (WEE). It is found that the *Brassica compestris* is a good Cadmium accumulator which holds the cadmium concentration in its leaves and roots in soil.

Keywords: Cadmium, Heavy metals, E-waste, *Channa punctatus, Brassica compestris*

INTRODUCTION

Among heavy metal pollutants, cadmium has been listed in "Black-list" of European community (Mason, 1996), and it is non-essential, non corrosive in nature and highly toxic metal which is distributed and released into the aquatic environment by anthropogenic sources. After India's independence, more and more mining and electrical industries has been established. Due to these industrial effluents, the concentration of cadmium and other heavy metals are increasing day by day in water and affecting aquatic flora and fauna. *Channa punctatus* is a fresh water fish and lives in depth of the water body. The cadmium leaches in the depth of water body absorbed by it and taken up as food by human. In living bodies cadmium causes various abnormalities and diseases. It is necessary to find the cheaper antagonist against cadmium contamination. *Brassica compestris* is a leafy herb and is the member of cruciferae family. It is used as dietary source of humans and fish also. It is a medicinal herb and its all parts are used in treatment of various types of diseases in humans.

HEAVY METALS: ENVIRONMENTAL TOXIC POLLUTANTS

The toxic metals are usually present in industrial, municipal and urban runoff which get incorporated into food chain and disturb the biochemical process occurring in the living body causing deformalities, diseases and even death are called environmental toxicants. The release of these toxic discharge especially heavy metals and pesticides, poses a threat to human life. These toxic pollutants are mainly Cadmium, Lead and Mercury is continuously affecting the aquatic environment. The above trio of heavy metals is an extremely important and serious problem that has attracted the attention of the scientists all over the world because they have disturbed the ecological balance at every aspect.

HEAVY METAL IS EMERGED AS A MAJOR CONCERN RELATED TO E-WASTES

Heavy metals cannot be destroyed or degraded. They enters through food chain in animal body and stored in different organs i.e., liver, kidney, muscles, gastrointestinal tract and blood. The exposure of cadmium in kidney of fish, led to changes of tubules began by deformation of brush border, gradual atrophy of basal cytoplasm and condensation of nuclear material following by focal necrosis of tubular cells and karyolysis and karyohexis is showed by Al-Mansoori, *et al.*, 2010 in their study.

The concentration of these heavy metals is increasing due to rapid increase of urbanization and industrialization in the form of Electronic and Electric Waste (WEE). E-waste is generated from any equipment, running on electricity or a battery that is discarded by the original user (still in working or non-working condition). UN has estimated amount of E-waste generated on the planet every year is 20-50 million tons and India is the fifth biggest generator of E-waste, discarding 1.7 million tones of WEE. The report has warned that the volume of global E-waste is likely to rise by 21 percent in next three years. Another analysis of TechNavio forecast the E-waste market in India 26.22 percent over the period of 2014-2019. India's E-waste is growing at the rate of 10% percent per annum and it constitutes 3-8% of municipal solid waste. Uttar Pradesh stands at fourth position among Indian states generating 10381.11 tons E-waste per year (Jayapradha, 2015). There are about 47 Indian recycling companies accounting only 27% recycling of E-waste leaving 83% just into the environment by which the concentration of heavy metals is continuously increasing and affecting flora and fauna, especially when we talk about aqua flora and fauna. It is very harmful for fishes.

CADMIUM TOXICITY AND ITS SOURCE

Cadmium is a silvery bluish-gray heavy metal and its symbol is Cd. The atomic number of Cadmium in periodic table is 48 has the atomic weight is 112.411 μCadmium ± 0.008 μ. The average concentration of cadmium in Earth's crust is between 0.1 and 0.5 ppm. Cadmium is a major pollutant of water and air comprising about 40% of total exposure. The major reason is developed countries are exporting their scrap of electronic and electric waste, in developing countries, like India because the availability of cheaper labor, high population density, lower environmental standards and high value of recovered raw material. Uncontrolled burning, disassembly and disposal of these goods cause a variety of environmental problems such as groundwater cadmium contamination. The EFSA Panel on Contaminants in the food Chain specifies that 2.5 μg/kg bodyweight is a tolerable weekly intake for humans (www.efsa.europa). The Joint FAO/WHO Expert Committee on Food Additives has declared 7 μg/kg bw to be the provisional tolerable weekly intake level (www.inchem.org).

In industries, cadmium occurs as a minor component in most zinc ores and therefore is a byproduct of zinc production. Cadmium was used for a long time as corrosion-resistant plating on steel and cadmium compounds are used as red, orange and yellow pigments, to color glass and to stabilize plastic. According to U.S. ATSDR - 1999, it is highly toxic metal which is distributed and released into the aquatic environment by industrial sources such as mining and refining of ores, Ni-Cd batteries, plating processes, the use of phosphate fertilizers and gasoline containing lead by fishery boats. According to an estimate 500 tones of cadmium enters the environment annually as a result of natural weathering and about 2000 tones is released annually as a result of human activities. The percentage of Cadmium found in E-waste in the form of large household appliances, Small household appliances and ICT and consumer electronics are 0.0014, 0.0068 and 0.018 respectively.

Due to poor discarding of E-waste, cadmium does not break down in the environment, remains in aquatic environments as well as remains in fish body for long periods of time and can bio-accumulate for many years after exposure to low levels of this metal. It has no biological function explained by Hogan & Michael, 2010. Fish may act as an organism for indicating the potential for exposure of human population to pollutants in water reservoir and recognized as major vectors for contaminant transfer to humans. The disease Itai-Itai resulting from consumption of cadmium contaminated rice in Japan is a well known case of cadmium toxicity is described by Hodgson, E. *et al.*, 2004.

CADMIUM TOXICITY IN *CHANNA PUNCTATUS*

The cadmium content was more in kidney> liver>gills in *Channa punctatus*. Cadmium decreased the glucose and total cholesterol level significantly ($P<0.001$ or $P<0.01$, as compared to the respective control value), without any significant change in SGPT, protein and triglyceride levels is observed by Arya and Sharma, 2015. Cadmium has a tangible effect on the protein and reduction in glycogen levels in certain tissues of fresh water fish, *Channa punctatus*, which may cause severe to fatal physio-metabolic dysfunctions. The cadmium treated fishes showed erratic swimming, loss of equilibrium, restlessness, sluggishness, jumping, opercular movements, Lastly they remained in a vertical position (Kawade and Khillare, 2014). Cadmium chloride exhibited several histological alterations like loosening, formation of clusters and lumps in haemopoietic tissue, deshaping of uriniferous tubules, narrowing of tubular lumen, vacuolization and degeneration of the cells of uriniferous tubules, increase of space in renal corpuscles and shrinking in glomeruli is found in their observation by Amin, *et al.*, 2013.

The chronic exposure to $CdCl_2$ in *Channa orientalis* increases TLC and decreases Hb content as compared to control group is reported by Borane,VR. 2013. Fishes are a good source of proteins and a staple food of many countries. *Channa punctatus* is a fresh water fish and have a high nutritional value and easily available in most of the areas. In India coastal areas like West Bengal, Goa, Kerala and other southern states, consumptions of the fishes is high.

Fishes can be used as biomarker for monitoring pollution in aquatic system. *Channa punctatus* can be cultured at below the standard level of its habitat and can be maintained easily. It is cheaper so research can be done on *C. punctatus* quite comfortable among other fresh water fishes. Due to *C. punctatus* burrows in mud and prefers stagnant and muddy to running waters, heavy metal concentration will be high and stored in it. Cadmium has a tremendous effect on physiology so brings about characteristics alterations in different functions of the vital organs such as kidney, liver, brain, heart, lung and tissues like muscle, skin, bone etc. It has been found that accumulation of cadmium in kidney causes renal tumors in 10-30% fishes.

Apart from their importance as a food fish, snakeheads are also consumed as a therapeutic for wound healing as well as reducing post-operative pain and discomfort, and collected for the international aquarium pet trade.

CADMIUM REMEDIATION AND ROLE OF *BRASSICA COMPESTRIS*

Neem leave powder NLP as adsorbent agent, its efficiently removes cadmium from water decreasing it in tissue of fish. While NLWE as detoxifying agent which remove cadmium in low degree but affect significantly the hematological, physiological and immunological state of *Oreochromis niloticus* improving health status of fish is investigated by Hussien and Asmaa, 2013.

Brassica compestris is the member of cruciferae family of order parietals of plant kingdom. It is used as vegetable, fodder and edible oil is extracted from its seeds. Mustard seeds used as spices. Its tender leaves and roots are generally used as culinary vegetable in the form of soup, sauce, etc. Rapeseed oil, to a small extent, is used in cooking. In India it is also mixed with Fuller's Earth and applied to the body, which strengthens before bathing, as a good, cool, substitute for soap. Oil is used in skin diseases. Pressed cake is suitable for feeding cattle; extracted cake is used as manure. *Brassica compestris* also has the medicinal value. Its seed is used in chronic bronchitis, cancer and tumors. Roots are used as emollient and diuretic. Its juice is used in chronic cough and bronchial catarrh. If mashed and mixed with bread and milk, it makes and excellent poultice for indolent sores. Green tops provide an excellent spring medicine. It is also used in treatment of snake-biting.

For control of heavy metals in water and fishes, we have to focus on cheaper and easier methods of remediation. It is predicted that the leafy vegetables hold the higher concentration of cadmium than other plants. Cadmium is easily taken up by plants and enters food chain resulting in a serious health issue for humans. *Brassica compestris* is also a leafy herb and also used as food stuff for fishes which accumulates the cadmium concentration 3.5-4.0 times more Cd concentration than the soil concentration is discussed by Lai *et al.*, 2013. It can be used against cadmium toxicity.

CONCLUSION

Cadmium chloride shows a marked change in their behavioural and morphological changes swimming, loss of equilibrium, restlessness, sluggishness, jumping, opercular movements and lastly they remained in a vertical position when exposed to various concentration. The toxic pollutant affects water quality and feeding, swimming behaviour of fish and also delays the hatching, maturation period (Atif *et al.*, 2005; Laovitthayanggoon 2006 and Kumar, 2007; Srivastava and Srivastava, 1998).

Experimental results of the Lai *et al.*, 2013 study showed that *Brassica compestris* is a cadmium accumulator which accumulated 3.5-4.0 times more cadmium concentration than the soil concentration. Once it was grown in the cadmium-contaminated soils, the cadmium concentrations in the edible parts kept at a constant level during different growth stages. Both leaf area and soil, cadmium concentrations play important roles regarding the accumulation of cadmiumin mustard.

REFERENCES

Al-Mansoori, A., Al-Ali, Balqis and Saoud, H.A. 2010: Effect of Cadmium and Lead Exposure and Recovery on Kidney of Fishes Juveniles *Carassius carassius* (L.) Journal of Thi-Qar University. Sp. No. Vol. 5: 40-50.

Amin, N., Manohar, S., Borana, K., Qureshi, TA and Khan, S. 2013: Effect of Cadmium Chloride on the Histoarchitecture of Kidney of a Freshwater Catfish, *Channa punctatus*. Jour. of Chemical, Biologicaland Physical Sciences. 3 (3): 1900-1905.

Arya, A. and Sharma, G.R. 2015: Combined Effects of Cadmium and Mercury on some Biochemical and Histolchemical Changes in Liver, Kidney and Gills of *Channa punctatus* (Bloch). Int. J. of Phar. Sciences. 7(8): 117-120.

Atif, F., Parvez, S., Pandey, S., Ali, M., Kaur, M., Rehman, H., Khan, H.A. and Raisuddin, S. (2005) Modulatory Effect of Cadmium Exposure on Deltamethrin-Induced Oxidative Stress in Channa Punctatus Bloch. Arch. Environ. Contam. Toxicol., 49: 371-377.

Borane, V.R. 2013: Protective Role of Ascorbic Acid on the Cadmium Chloride induced Changes in Hematology of the Freshwater Fish, *Channa orientalis* (Schncider). Advances in Applied Science Research. 4(2): 305-308.

Hodgson, E., Cope, W.G. and Leidy B.R. 2004: Classes of Toxicants: Use Classes. In A Textbook of Modern Toxicology (Ed: 3rd). John Wiley & Sons. Inc., Hoboken. New Jersey. P: 52.

Hogan, C. and Michael (2010). Heavy metal. Encyclopedia of Earth. National Council for Science and the Environment. E. Monosson and C. Cleveland (eds.). Washington DC.

Http://www.efsa.europa.eu/en/efsajournal/pub/2551.html

Http://www.inchem.org/documents/jecfa/jeceval/jec_297.html

Hussein, A.M.O. and Asmaa M. H. 2013: Removal of Cadmium from Freshwater Cultured Nile tilapia *Oreochtromis niloticus* using Neem Leave Water Extract (NLWE) and Neem Leave Powder (NLP). Nature and Sciences. 11 (12).

Jayapradha, A. 2015: Scenario of E-waste in India and Application of New Recycling Approaches for E-waste Management. J. of Chemical and Pharmaceutical Res. 7(3): 232-238.

Kawade, S. and Khillare, Y. 2014: Studies on Toxicity and Behavioural Responses under Cadmium Stress in *Channa punctatus* (Bloch.). The Int. J. of Sci. and Tech. 2(13): 71-75.

Kumar, P., Prasad, Y. & Patra, A.K. (2007) Levels of Cadmium and Lead in Tissues of Freshwater Fish (Clarias batrachus L.) and Chicken in Western U.P. (India). Bull Environ Contam Toxicol., 79: 396-400.

Lai, Hung-Yu and Chen, Bo-Ching. 2013: The Dynamic Growth Exhibition and Accumulation of Cadmium of Pak Choi (*Brassica campestris* L. ssp. *chinensis*) Grown in Contaminated Soils. Int. J. Environ. Res. Public Health 10: 5284-5298.

Laovitthyanggoon, S. (2006) Effects of Cadmium Level on Chromosomal Structure of Snakehead-fish (Ophiocephalus stiatus). Fac. of Guard. Studies, Mahidol Univ. Thailand.

Mason, C. F. (1996) Biology of Freshwater Pollution., III Ed., Longman, U.K. 1-4.

Srivastav, S.K. & Srivastav, A.K. (1998) Annual Changes in Serum Calcium and Inorganic Phosphate Levels and Correlation with Gonadal Status of Freshwater Murrel, Channa punctatus (Bloch). Brazillian J. Of Medical and Boil. Res., 31: 1069-1073.

USATSDR (United States Agency for Toxic Substances Disease Registry) (1999) Toxicological Profile for Cadmium. Published by U.S. Department of Health and the Human Services. Public Health Services., 229-240.

Pages: **81-90**

Renewable Resources and Environment
Edited by: **Dr. Baby Tabassum**
ISBN: 978-93-5056-893-4
Edition: **2018**
Published by: **Discovery Publishing House Pvt. Ltd., New Delhi (India)**

Solar Energy in India
Present Status Barrier and Future Potential

Raju

ABSTRACT

The demand for energy is increasing day by day in the whole world. The Conventional energy sources like coal and petroleum are limited. Renewable energy resources will play an important role in the future. India is situated in sunny belt India is gifted with vast solar energy potential. Government of India had launched Jawaharlal Nehru National Solar Mission (JNNSM) in 2009. The target was to start Grid connected Solar Projects of 20 GW by 2022. In May 2015 government increases the target to 100 GW by 2022. This study provides an overview on solar energy in India. It reviews the current status of solar energy in terms of existing capacity, along with historical trends of solar energy. Thisstudy also focus on the technical and financial barriers and challenges for development and utilization of solar energy technology. This study reviews existing government act and regulatory policies to support solar energy development in India. Indicating how these policies are helping in achieving their goals. Finally, a review based on of the future target of solar energy supply has been presented.

Dept. of Physics Govt. Raza P.G. College, Rampur (U.P.) (India)

INTRODUCTION

Electricity is very important for any country for urbanization, industrialization, economic growth and improvement of living standard of society. India is ranked fifth in the electricity generation in the world. Presently, India has installed capacity of 276.783 GW out of which 69.6% is from thermal, 15.2% from hydro, 2.1% from nuclear and about 13.2% from renewable energy sources (as on August 2015). Table 8.1 shows the electricity requirement and availability in India. Thus, Indian power sector is basically based on fossil fuels, with about three-fifths of the country's power is generating by reserves of coal. The thermal power station emit a high amount of toxic gases such as NOx, COx and SOx gases which is ingenious to health and environment. In last few decades' Indian government has taken many steps to reduce the use of fossil fuels-based energy and promote renewable energy generation.

Table 8.1

The electricity sector requirement and availability in India on March 2015

	Energy in MU	Peak in MW
Availability	1,030,785	141,160
Requirement	1,068,923	148,166
Shortage	38,138	7,006
Percentage shortage	3.6	4.7

India was the first country in the world to set up a Ministry of non-conventional energy resources in early 1980. The Solar and wind energy are freely available and they are environment friendly. The wind energy systems are not possible at all sites because of low wind speeds and it is more unpredictable than solar energy. Solar energy is the most important renewable energy resource which is available in most of the country of the world. Even its technically available potential is much higher than the current total primary energy demand. Solar energy technology is very important tool which can lowers worldwide carbon emissions. The cost of solar energy technologies are rapid declining in the recent past years and it is showing potential for continuous declines in the near future. Currently, the installed capacity of solar energy projects in India is about 4.22 GW. India is planning to produce 100 GW of solar power by 2022.

SOLAR POWER IN INDIA

Overview of Solar Power

Solar power can be generated by direct photovoltaic's (PV) or indirect by solar thermal power. In photovoltaic power plant a solar cell or photovoltaic cell (PV) is used which is a device that converts light into electric power using the photoelectric effect.

The PV cell is a solid-state device consists of thin layers of Semiconductor materials that produce electricity when exposed to light. Photovoltaic power generation consist of solar panels having a number of solar cells containing some photovoltaic materials. Materials presently used for photovoltaic are mono-crystalline silicon, poly-crystalline silicon, cadmium telluride and copper indium selenide/sulfide. The International Energy Agency has classified the photovoltaic applications into four categories namely off-grid domestic, off-grid nondomestic, grid connected distributed and grid connected centralized. In a Concentrating Solar Power (CSP) plant the heat is collected by lenses or mirrors and transformed to mechanical energy through a steam turbine and then into electricity. Wide ranges of technologies CSP plant are present; the most developed are parabolic trough, solar power tower, concentrating linear Fresnel reflector and sterling dish. The various techniques are used to track the sun and focus light. here we will discuss both type plants in India.

Solar Power in India

India lies in the sunny belt of the world. India is endowed with vast solar energy potential. Most parts of India get 300 days of sunshine a year. About 5,000 trillion kWh per year energy is incident over Indian land area with most area receiving 4-7 kWh per sq. meter per day. Hence, both technology solar thermal and solar photovoltaic's can effectively provide huge capability for solar in India. Solar also provides the ability to generate power on a distributed basis. Assuming 10% conversion efficiency for PV modules it is three orders of magnitude greater than the likely electricity demand for India on the year 2015. Figure 8.1 shows solar radiation data map of India. It can be observed that highest annual global radiation is received in Rajasthan and northern Gujarat.

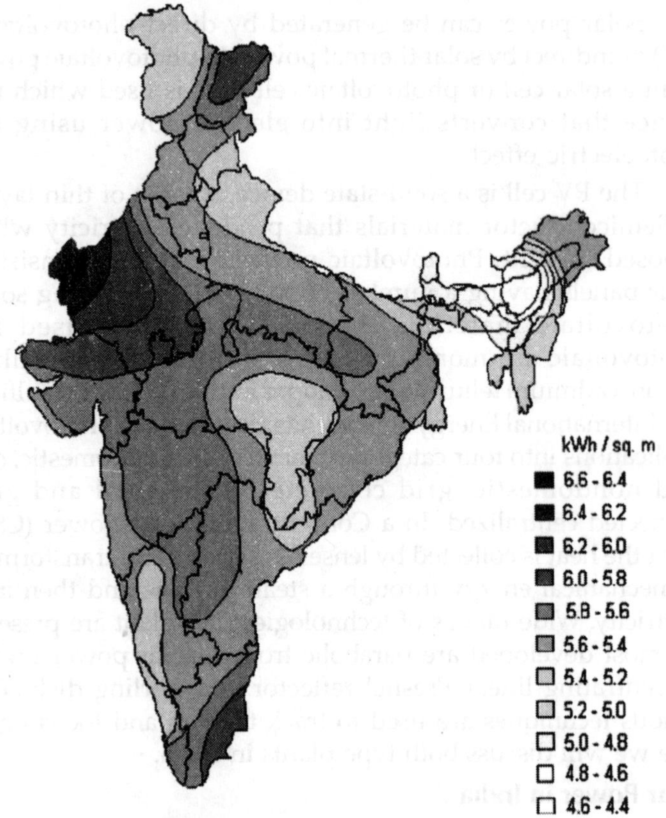

Fig. 8.1: Solar radiation map of India

Current Status of Solar Energy in India

India is ranked 11th in solar power generation in the world as on Jan. 2014. Government funded solar energy in India only accounted for about 6.4MW/yr of power as of 2005. In 2010 capacity of 25.1MW was added and 468.3 MW in 2011. In 2012 the capacity increase more than two times and become 1205 MW. During 2013 capacity added by 4MW and during 2014 capacity added by 313MW. In August 2015, the installed grid connected solar power capacity is 4.22 GW. The price of solar energy has come down from Rs. 17.90 per unit in 2010 to about Rs. 7 per unit in 2015. It is expected that with technology improvement and market competition solar power will reach grid parity by 2017-18[13]. The Grid parity means the cost of electricity generated from alternative energy becomes equal or less than the cost of purchasing power from the grid. Grid parity is very important term in the solar system and preferably photovoltaic panel. The Charanka Solar Park[16], at current installed capacity of 224 MW is the largest Solar Park in Asia, was commissioned on April 19, 2012. Some solar power plant of India is shown in the table 8.2. In India, Rajasthan has the largest share of solar power generation of 28.4% and Gujarat share is 24.4% as on September 2015. Table 8.3 shows current solar power capacity in different state of India.

Table 8.2

Some solar plants of India

Name of Plant	Peak Power in MW	Commission Year
Charanka Solar Park, Charanka village, Patan, Gujarat	224	April 2012
Welspun Solar MP project, Neemuch, Madhya Pradesh	151	March 2013
Mahagenco Solar Project, Maharashtra	130	March 2013
Rajgarh Solar PV (NTPC), Rajghar Madhya Pradesh	50	March 2014
Welspun Energy Rajasthan Solar Project, Phalodhi, Rajasthan	50	March 2013
Talcher Kaniha Solar PV (NTPC), Odisha	10	March 2014
Unchahar Solar PV(NTPC), Unchahar Utter Pradesh	10	March 2014

Table 8.3

Current solar power capacity in some state as on September 2015

S.No.	State	Capacity in MW
1.	Andhra Pradesh	279.44
2.	Arunachal Pradesh	0.265
3.	Chhattisgarh	73.18
4.	Gujarat	1000.05
5.	Haryana	12.8
6.	Jharkhand	16
7.	Karnataka	104.22
8.	Kerala	12.025
9.	Madhya Pradesh	673.58
10.	Maharashtra	378.7
11.	Orissa	56.92
12.	Punjab	200.32
13.	Rajasthan	1199.7
14.	Tamil Nadu	157.98
15.	Telangana	72.25
16.	Tripura	5
17.	Uttar Pradesh	71.26
18.	Uttarakhand	5
19.	West Bengal	7.21
20.	Andaman & Nicobar	5.1
21.	Delhi	6.712
22.	Lakshadweep	0.75
23.	Puducherry	0.025
24.	Chandigarh	5.041
25.	Daman & Diu	2.5
26.	Others	0.79
	Total	4346.818

CHALLENGES ON SOLAR ENERGY IN INDIA

Various barriers and challenges on solar energy in India have been pointed below:

- The main disadvantage of solar energy is its unavailability. The weather conditions are major factor on availability of solarradiation. So, we can't say in a particular time the energy from solar will be available to us or not.
- Land is also a secret reserve in India and as per capital availability is low. Large land area is required, which sometimes is not feasible. The amount of land required for utility-scale solar power plants is currently approximately 1km2 for every 20-60MW generation.
- 100 GW of solar would mean about 10.5% share for solar power in total generation of power in India. Such large share of intermittent sources requires huge investments in the power grid infrastructure for transmission smart supply and demand management.
- To achieve a capacity of 60 GW for utility scale projects by 2022, there would be a requirement of about $40 billion. The government currently expects a big share of this to come from international sources. But an international fund for solar projects in India is very less.
- Storage problem is also very serious. Suppose if the demand of power is not so high then the electricity produced by the solar plant will have to be stored somewhere to supply when demanded. This increases the cost of the project

INDIAN GOVERNMENT INCENTIVES AND SUPPORT

Government acts and policies Government of India has come out with Acts and Policies to support renewable Energy.

- The Electricity Act 2003 has promoted electricity generation from co-generation and renewable energy sources. This Act accelerated the process of renewable energy development in the country. The guidelines for competitive procurement have been framed under Section 63 of the Electricity Act 2003 it states.

- "The Appropriate Commission shall adopt the tariff if such tariff has been determined through transparent process of bidding in accordance with the guidelines issued by the Central Government".
- The National Electricity Policy 2005 stipulates that the share of electricity from non- conventional resources would need to be increased such purchase by distribution companies shall be through competitive process.
- According to Tariff Policy 2006 states the Appropriate Commission shall decide a minimum percentage for purchase of energy from non- conventional source according the availability of resources in that region and its impact on retail tariffs.

Government Support

The Government of India is providing Rs. 15,050 cr. subsidy to promote solar capacity addition in the country. This capital subsidy will be provided for solar projects in many cities and towns. Solar power projects with investment of about Rs. 90,000cr. would be developed using bundling method with thermal Power. Further, investment will come from large Public Sector

Undertakings (PSU) and Independent Power Producers (IPPs). Many states Government have also come out with state solar policies to promote solar energy technology.

CONCLUSION

Here we have discussed about the current status of solar energy in India. The Ministry of non- convection energy resources, government of India is trying to increases the power capacity and achieve the target of 100 GW by 2022. This discussion shows that the status of solar energy is satisfactory in India but some extra effort is required for betterment of solar source. In spite of reduction of the cost of solar power, it is expensive source of power compared with conventional sources. It is very important to support and subsidize the solar power till it can compete with the conventional sources. The step of Indian government to increases the target is a very good to become India as one of the most solar powered countries in the world. Such types of steps will be required in the future.

REFERENCES

A Discussion Paper, Barriers to Development of Renewable Energy in India & Proposed Recommendation. Infrastructure Development Finance Company Ltd. 2010.

Amita U and Soni MS. Concentrating Solar Power – Technology, Potential and Policy in India. Renewable and Sustainable Energy Reviews. 2011; 15: 5161-5175.

Ashok U and Arnab C. Solar Energy Fundamentals and Challenges in Indian Restructured Power Sector. International Journal of Scientific and Research Publications. 2014; 4: 1-13.

Atul S. A Comprehensive Study of Solar Power in India and World. Renewable and Sustainable Energy Review. 2011; 15: 1767-1777.

Dubey S and Chamoli S. Indian Scenario of Solar Energy and its Application in Cooling Systems: A Review. International Journal of Engineering Research and Technology. 2013; 6: 571-578.

https://en.wikipedia.org/wiki/Solar_power_in_India

https://en.wikipedia.org/wiki/Grid_parity

https://en.wikipedia.org/wiki/Gujarat_Solar_Park

http://www.welspun.com/energy.asp

https://en.wikipedia.org/wiki/NTPC_Limited

India Solar Handbook: Bridge to India. Bridge to India Energy Pvt. Ltd, India. 2015.

Information Bureau. Ministry of New and Renewable Energy, Government of India.

Ishan P and Pallav P. Techno-economic Evaluation of Concentrating Solar Power Generation in India. Energy Policy. 2010; 38: 3015-3039.

Jawaharlal Nehru National Solar Mission, Press Information Bureau. Ministry of New and Renewable Energy, Government of India.

Krithika PR and Siddha M. Background Paper Governance of Renewable Energy in India: Issues and Challenges. TERI-NEFI. 2014.

Load Generation and Balance Report, Central Electricity Authority, Ministry of Power, Government of India. Central Electricity Authority. 2015-16.

Lolla S and Roy SB. Wind and Solar Resources in India. Energy Procedia. 2015; 70: 187-192.

Ojha AK and Gaur GK. Solar Energy and Economic Development in India: A Review. International Journal of Emerging Technology and Advanced Engineering. 2014; 4: 184-189.

Ongoing and Future Power Projects, Mahagenco Maharashtra State Power Generation Co. Ltd. Maharashtra.

Pidaparthi AS and Prasad NR. India's First Solar Thermal Parabolic trough Pilot Power Plant. Energy Procedia. 2014; 49: 1840-1847.

Power Sector at a Glance all India, Ministry of Power, Government of India. 2015.

Rachit S, Vinod KG, Solar Power – Current Status, Challenges and Policies in India. Research & Reviews: Journal of Engineering and Technology, Volume 5.

Renewable Energy in India: Growth and Targets Ministry of New and Renewable Energy (MNRE), Government of India, 2015.

Sharma BD. Performance of Solar Power Plants in India. Central Electricity Regulatory Commission New Delhi. 2011.

Solar Energy in India, Solar Energy Association, Tamil Nadu.

Solar, Ministry of New and Renewable Energy, Government of India. Revision of Cumulative Targets under National Solar Mission from 20,000 MW by 202122 to 1,00,000 MW, Press.

State wise Installed Solar Power Capacity, Ministry of New and Renewable Energy, Government of India.

The Electricity Act, 2003. The Gazette of India.

Vikas K and Gupta BL. Grid Parity for Solar Energy in India. International Conference on Emerging Trends in Engineering and Technology. TMU Moradabad. 2012.

Vikas K, *et al*. Status of Solar Wind Renewable Energy in India. Renewable and Sustainable Energy Reviews. 2013; 27: 1-10.

Pages: **91-98**

Renewable Resources and Environment
Edited by: Dr. Baby Tabassum
ISBN: 978-93-5056-893-4
***Edition:* 2018**
***Published by:* Discovery Publishing House Pvt. Ltd., New Delhi (India)**

Role of Solar Energy Technologies in Sustainable Development

Dr. Shraddha Gupta

ABSTRACT

Renewable energy technologies are substantially safer than any other conventional energy sources in context with the environmental and social issues. Sustainable energy is the energy that, in its production or consumption, has minimal negative impacts on human health and the healthy functioning of vital ecological systems, including the global environment. It is an accepted fact that renewable energy is a sustainable form of energy, which has attracted more attention during recent years. Increasing environmental interest, as well as economic consideration of fossil fuel consumption and high emphasis of sustainable development for the future helped to bring the great potential of renewable energy into focus.

Sustainable development is generally defined as development that meets the needs of the present without compromising the ability of future generations to meet their own needs. To evaluate potential of renewable energy technology we have to concern with energy, transport, agriculture, water and industry sectors. Study reveals that the energy sector is the most prominent example, where the countries need to increase their capacity substantially and, at

---

Department of Physics, Government PG College, Budaun - 243 601 (U.P.) (India)
email: shraddha.phy@gmail.com

the same time, replace old outdated plants with new eco-efficient technologies. This paper underline the need to assess both the social and environmental impacts of solar energy technologies to ensure that renewable energy deployment remains aligned with overall sustainable development goals.

Keywords: Renewable energy, Solar energy and Sustainable development.

INTRODUCTION

Traditionally, sustainability has been framed in the three-pillar model: Economy, Ecology and Society are all considered to be interconnected and relevant for sustainability [1]. The three-pillar model explicitly acknowledges the encompassing nature of the sustainability concept and allows a schematic categorization of sustainability issues. The United Nations General Assembly aims for action to promote the integration of the three components of SD–economic development, social development and environmental protection–as interdependent and mutually reinforcing pillar [2]. This view subscribes to an understanding where a certain set of actions (e.g., substitution of fossil fuels with RE sources) can fulfill all three development goals simultaneously. Sustainability is the approach of India towards growth and development [3]. Solar Energy is one of the sectors that are recognized to support the sustainability of India. Solar energy has giant potential in India due to its position in tropical belt [4, 5].

SOLAR ENERGY

In modern age energy consumption has reached an alarming level. The total primary energy consumption from crude oil (26.45%), natural gas (6.7%), coal (54.6%), nuclear energy (1.26%), hydro electricity (5.0%), wind power, biomass electricity and solar power is 595 Mtoe in the year 2015 [6]. Due to rapid economic expansion, India has one of the world's fastest growing energy markets and is expected to be the second-largest contributor to the increase in global energy demand by 2035, accounting for 18% of the rise in global energy consumption.

Table 9.1

Current use and current potentials of selected renewable energy sources [7]

Resource	Current Use	Technical Potential	Theoretical Potential
Hydropower	9	50	147
Biomass energy	50	276	2900
Solar energy	0.1	1575	3900000
Wind energy	0.12	640	6000

Units: Exajoule per year

Amongst the different renewable energies that have to be developed, solar energy is a candidate with high potential. Indeed, the energy supply from the sun is quite enormous: on an average, the solar power received on the Earth's surface during one hour is equivalent to the energy demand of the human population during a whole year [8]. From the point of view of eco-physics only those energy sources that contaminate the environment minimally are acceptable. The cleanest source of energy is the sun whose irradiation is free of charge and more or less accessible to the whole Earth and the Solar system.

The application of solar energy can be classified as two different groups – Photovoltaic (PV) and Solar Thermal. Some applications of solar energy is shown in figure 9.1.

With the emergence of industry and the increase in energy consumption, the problem of the quality of environment is getting bigger. World is faced with the problem of contamination and environment pollution including higher layers of atmosphere and the ozone layer. In our previous paper [9] we have studied energy consumption and material used (or byproducts) in the whole life of a PV system. The manufacture of photovoltaic modules uses some hazardous materials which can present health and safety hazards, if adequate precautions are not taken. Routine conditions in manufacturing facilities should not pose any threats to health and the environment. Such hazards arise primarily from the toxicity and explosiveness of specific gases.

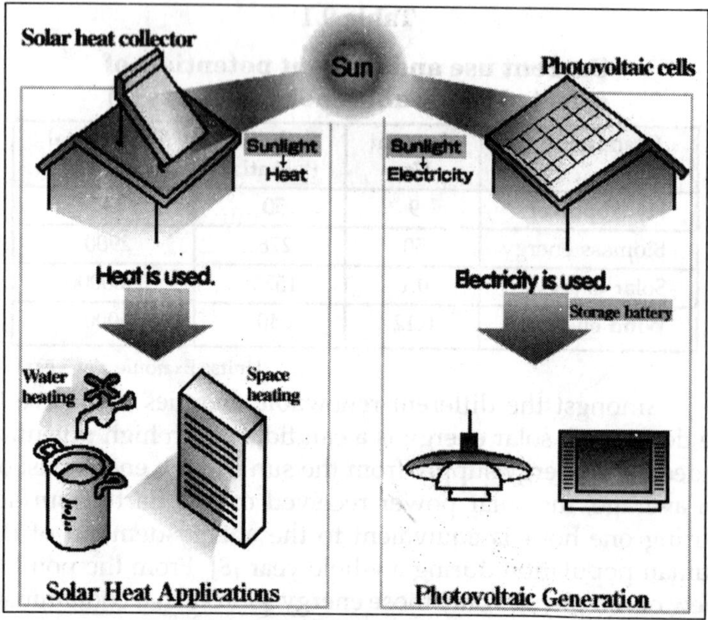

Fig. 9.1: Some applications of solar energy

If we choose safer technologies, processes, and materials, better use of materials, and by employee training, safety procedures and follow some quality parameters, its negative impacts is minimized.

SUSTAINABLE DEVELOPMENT

A notion of the sustainable development is defined as an integral economic, technological, social and cultural development adjusted to the needs of the environment protection, which enables current and future generations to meet their needs and improve their life quality. Sustainable development is focused on the preservation of the natural eco-systems and on the rational use of the natural treasures of the Earth. Thus this concept is oriented towards the upgrading of the life and environment quality. Sustainable development implies nature preservation by man on sustainable basis and its use to the extent of its reproduction. Overuse and uncontrolled use and exploitation of the natural resources can cause a violation of the ecological balance and thus ecological disasters as well.

The basic principle of sustainable development is that natural resources can be exploited only to the level that provides their reproduction. This idea encompasses interregional and intergeneration equality. Problem of sustainability comprises several aspects: energy consumption, population, agriculture and biodiversity, global warming and contamination, equality in the use of resources and urbanism.

Guidelines given in Agenda of COP 21 to continue the way towards a sustainable development [10] are:

(a) Regarding resource preservation:
  - use of natural resources should be based on rational use of land;
  - saving wise use of non-renewable energy sources and their substitution by the renewable energy resources whenever possible;
  - maintenance and protection of biological balance;

(b) Regarding environment quality:
  - It is essential to prevent or diminish degrading processes or those that contaminate environment in order to protect regenerating abilities of ecosystems and to prevent development dangerous to human health or diminishes the quality of life.

ROLE OF SOLAR ENERGY IN SUSTAINABLE DEVELOPMENT

Solar Energy is one of the renowned sectors to support the sustainability of India. Solar energy has giant potential in India due to its position in tropical belt. The role of solar energy for sustainable development can be viewed in different field as

- Solar in Transportation
- Solar Lighting
- Solar Mobile/I-Pad Charger
- Solar Car parking
- Solar Kitchen Restaurant
- Solar Bill Board
- Solar Canal

- Solar Space Power Station
- Solar in Architecture

The installed capacity in India can be understood by analyzing the solar energy produced in recent past years in various states of the country [11].

Table 9.2

State wise Installed Capacity of Solar Projects under various Schemes as on 15/12/2014

State	Total Commissioned Capacity (MW)	% Contribution
Andhra Pradesh	234.86	7.821731
Arunachal Pradesh	0.025	0.000833
Chhattisgarh	7.6	0.253109
Gujarat	929.05	30.9409
Haryana	12.8	0.426289
Jharkhand	16	0.532861
Karnataka	67	2.231355
Kerala	0.025	0.000833
Madhya Pradesh	353.58	11.77556
Maharashtra	286.9	9.554861
Orissa	31.5	1.04907
Punjab	55.77	1.857353
Rajasthan	839.5	27.95854
Tamil Nadu	104.2	3.470256
Telangana	8	0.26643
Uttar Pradesh	29.51	0.982795
Uttarakhand	5	0.166519
West Bengal	7.21	0.24012
Andaman & Nicobar	5.1	0.169849
Delhi	5.465	0.182005
Lakshadweep	0.75	0.024978
Puducherry	0.025	0.000833
Chandigarh	2	0.066608
Others	0.79	0.02631
Total	3062.68	100

CHALLENGES IN SUSTAINABLE DEVELOPMENT

In order to establish sustainable development, prevent over consumption of conventional energy sources and to preserve environment it is necessary to provide for sustainable energetic.

- Lack of electricity supply or steady electricity
- Lack of clean potable water supply in:
  - Rural areas
  - Agriculture
- Lack of communication media
- Lack of health services and education system
- Lack of fuel supply for cooking applications
- Insufficient grid infrastructure
- Government policy planning and financial assistance.

This means that future technical-technological development should be based on the strict control and lowering of the pollutant emission into the environment, extended use of eco-technologies and renewable energy resources.

CONCLUSION

Solar energy is the best solution in bridging India's energy demand-supply gap in the future. It is clear that the alternatives of solar energy are going to be immensely more costly. In transportation industry solar vechiles like solar car, solar bus, solar rail, solar boat, solar aircraft and solar roadways are applications for sustainable development in India. Solar lighting, solar mobile charger, solar car parking, solar kitchen restaurant, solar bill board, solar canal, solar space power station, solar in architecture are the some other innovative application for sustainable development of India. To promote solar energy research and development capacity have to be built in the private sector and in educational institutions. Millions of productive jobs will be created in the process of development of the infrastructure required for the new industries resulting from massive solar projects.

REFERENCES

1. Bojö, J., K.-G. Maler, and L. Unemo (1992). *Environment and Development: An Economic Approach.* Kluwer Academic Publishers, Dordrecht, The Netherlands and Boston, MA, USA.
2. *World Summit Outcome. Resolution Adopted by the General Assembly.* A/RES/60/1, United Nations, New York, NY, USA *2005.*
3. Approach Paper to Twelfth Five Year Plan, 2012-2017. Available from: http://planningcommission.nic.in/plans/planrel/12appdrft/appraoch_12plan.pdf. Retrieved 2016-02-09.
4. Muneer T, Asif M, Munnawar M. Sustainable Production of Solar Electricity with Particular Reference to Indian Economy. *Renew Sustain Energy Rev.* 2005; 9(5): 444-73.
5. Ramachandra TV, Jain R, Krishnadas G. Hotspots of Solar Potential in India. *Renew Sustain Energy Rev.* 2011; 15(6): 3178-3186.
6. *Statistical Review of world energy 2015* Retrieved 17 June 2015.
7. United Nations Development Programme (UNDP) World Energy Assessment, ISBN 92-1-126126-0, New York (2011).
8. T. Markvart, *Solar Electricity,* 2nd ed. (John Wiley & Sons, 2010). ISBN 0-471-98853-7.
9. Ratna Sircar, Shraddha Gupta, Jyotsana Trivedi, Dibya Prakash Srivastava, *"Environmental Impact of Thin Film Silicon Solar Cell"* 3rd Lucknow Science Congress (LUSCON) – 2015 & National Conference on Science for Society, held at BBAU Lucknow on 31st Oct.-2nd Nov. 2015.
10. Naim H. Afgan *et al.*, Sustainable Energy Development, Renewable and Sustainable Energy Review 2, (1998) pp. 235-286.
11. Goldman DP, McKenna JJ, Murphy LM. Financing Projects that use Clean-energy Technologies: An Overview of Barriers and Opportunities. NREL/TP-600-38723. Golden, CO: National Renewable Energy Laboratory 2005. http://www.nrel.gov/docs/fy06osti/38723. pdf at 22:53, Retrieved 2015-02-12.

Pages: 99-106

Renewable Resources and Environment
Edited by: Dr. Baby Tabassum
ISBN: 978-93-5056-893-4
Edition: **2018**
Published by: **Discovery Publishing House Pvt. Ltd., New Delhi (India)**

Effect of Photoperiod and Testosterone Propionate Hormone on Body Mass and Testicular Volume in Brahminy Myna

Arvind Kumar

ABSTRACT

Three groups of adult male photosensitive brahminy myna birds were subjected to short day length (SDL) for a period of 30 days and then transferred to LDL for next 30 days. This experiment began on 20 January 2006. First group received olive oil (0.1 ml) on alternate days, served as control. Birds of group 2 and 3 received alternate dose of TP i.e. 50 and 100 µg per bird. Each symbol represents the mean and the vertical line on it indicates the standard error. Body mass and testicular volumes were collected at the beginning and at end of the experiment. The observation of this study was that effect of photoperiod and testosterone propionate on male brahminy myna at 50 µg TP can induce testicular growth in short day length and also testicular growth significantly increase under 100 µg TP per bird in LDLS.

Keywords: Male photosensitive brahminy myna, SDL, LDL, Testosterone propionate, testis.

INTRODUCTION

In seasonally breeding animals, the breeding season is restricted to the optimum period for raising young, which

Dept. of Zoology, Govt. Girls Degree College Badaun (U.P.) (India)
email: zooaayush@gmail.com

varies widely to suit the ecological needs of each species. In most species of birds from temperate latitudes, in which reproduction usually beings sometime during spring, the breeding season ends by the development of a state of photorefractoriness which results in spontaneous gonadal collapse and loss of response to stimulatory daylengths; once the birds are photorefractory, exposure for a time to short daylengths is necessary to render them photosensitive again. Similar results have been found in some spring/summer breeders that reproduce at high latitudes but overwinter in the tropics. Few birds are reported to undergo spontaneous gonadal regression under continuous long daylengths.

The recovery of photosensitivity in absolute photorefractory birds require a brief exposure to short days (winter days in nature) (Farner *et al.*, 1983). However, in a few species like mallard and tree sparrow photorefractoriness is terminated after prolonged exposure to long days, although short day may accelerate the process. In males of many birds, territorial behaviors, such as song and aggressive displays, are regulated by the hormone, testosterone (Hirschenhauser *et al.*, 2003). In general, circulating plasma levels of testosterone (T) increase in early spring from baseline levels of 0.1-0.2 ng/ml to about 2-10 ng/ml and then remain elevated throughout most of the reproductive period (Wingfield and Farner, 1993). In male song birds suppression of sickness behavior could occur when testosterone (T) is elevated to socially-modulated levels (Ashley *et al.*, 2009).

Role of gonadal steroids in the regulation of gonadal cycles has been studied in several Indian birds (Kumar *et al.*, 2009; Kumar 2013; Sharma *et al.*, 2007; Pandey and Bhardwaj 2015). Studies on these species have revealed that, depending on the species, on the phase of the gonadal cycles, and on the dose administered, testosterone may stimulate, inhibit or produce no effect on gonadal cycles of Indian birds. The gonadotrophin-inhibitory hormone (GnIH) and its related peptides are important modulators of reproductive function at the level of the GnRH neurone, the gonadotroph and the gonads (Bentley *et al.*, 2009).

MATERIAL AND METHODS

Experiment was performed in the photoperiodic chambers of the laboratory. During artificial photostimulation groups of birds were held in light – tight boxes lit by compact fluorescent tubes (CFL, Phillips) of 14 watt of an intensity of ~ 600 lux at perch level. Automatic time switches (Muller clock) controlled the periods of light and dark. In caged condition, birds were kept in small groups of (size – 45 × 30 × 30 cm) were placed in the photoperiodic box (size – 75 × 70 × 60 cm) for photoperiodic experiments. All birds were individually weighed on a portable top pan balance to the nearest 0.1g to record the changes in body mass. For this, the birds were individually wrapped in small cotton bag and weighed before being laparotomized. Food and water were available ad libitum. Testicular volume was calculated from the Bissonnette's formula i.e. $V = 4/3p ab^2$, where V is the volume, a is half of the long axis and b is the radius of the testis at its widest point. Results were analysed using 1 way RM ANOVA. Significance was always taken at $P < 0.05$. Data from these measurements were collected at the beginning and after 30 and 60 days of the experiment.

EXPERIMENT

This experiment was performed on photosensitive, adult male brahminy myna procured locally at 29°N. This experiment began on 20 January 2006. Three groups (1-3) of birds (n = 4 to 5) were subjected to SDL (8L:16D), for a period of 30 days and received 0.1 ml olive oil, 50 µg and 100 µg Testosterone propionate male hormone per bird on alternate day respectively and then transferred to LDL for next 30 days. In total, fifteen injection were made. Body mass and testicular volume were studied in this experiment. Observations were made at the beginning and end of the 30 day of the experiment.

RESULT

The results are shown in figure 10.1. The mean body mass was slightly increased after 30 days among all the three groups, exposed to 8L:16D (One way RM ANOVA BM olive oil (control group), $F_{2,6} = 0.6714$, P=0.5456; 50µg TP, $F_{2,6} = 2.219$, P=0.1900;

100μg TP, $F_{2,6}$ = 1.100, P = 8.3918) (fig. 10.1a). The testis volume of group 2 and 3 received 50μg and 100μg TP respectively was significantly stimulated and then transferred to LDL for next 30 days then the testis volume of 100μg TP group was more significantly stimulated. So there was a significant difference in testis volume of both group (One way RM ANOVA TV olive oil (control group), $F_{2,6}$ = 19.53, P=0.0024; 50μg TP, $F_{2,6}$ = 803.8, P<0.0001; 100μg TP, $F_{2,6}$ = 320.1, P<0.0001) (fig. 10.1b).

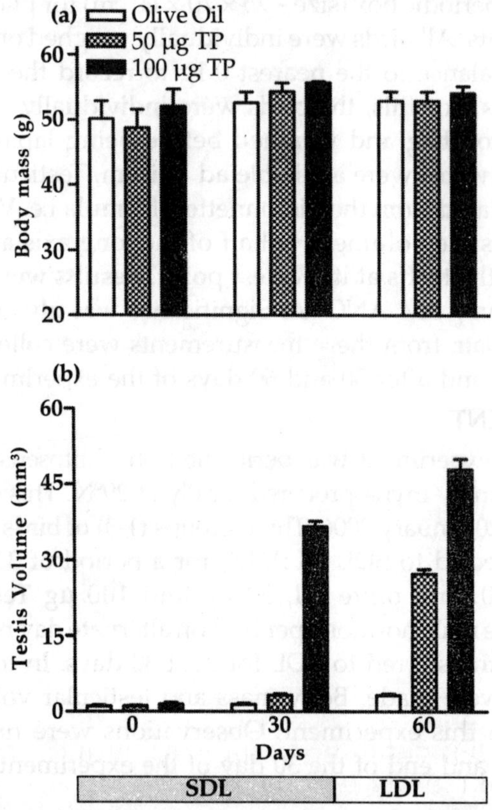

Fig. 10.1: Mean (±SE) of body mass (a) and testis volume (b) of birds (n=4-5) exposed to SDL for a period of 30 days and then transferred to LDL for next 30 days. First group received olive oil (0.1 ml) on alternate days, served as control. Birds of group 2 and 3 received alternate dose of TP i.e. 50 and 100 μg per bird. Each symbol represents the mean and the vertical line on it indicates the standard error

DISCUSSION

In the post-breeding phase, testes of all control birds were very small and in the state of regression. Testosterone treatment during the period when the gonads were inactive did not affect the testis weight. It is suggested that the differential effect of exogenous TP on the testes are due to its dose–dependent action (Turek, *et al.*, 1976). In Western Scrub-Jays (Aphelocoma californica) birds with unpredictable food had slightly lower testosterone levels relative to controls, but there was no effect on estradiol or luteinizing hormone (Bridge *et al.*, 2009). Effect of TP has also been investigated in the migratory red headed bunting, Emberiza bruniceps (Kumar and Kumar, 1990). TP declines food intake but dose not potentially affect the gain in fat and body mass. This suggested that photoperiodic effects on fattening and weight gain in Emberiza bruniceps were not exerted through hyperphagia. Kumaran and Turner (1949) and Lofts (1962) suggested that the testosterone had no adverse effect on gonads in near maximum breeding condition, but spermatocytes. It is also suspected that the spermatokinetic effect of exogenous androgen is by way of direct action of the hormone on the testis. Brown and Follett (1977) showed that testosterone induced spermatokinetic effect was lost when birds were hypophysectomized before treatment, and thus demonstrated the role of pituitary factors(s) in the stimulatory action of this androsteroid. Studied performed by Davies and Bicknell (1976) and others on different avian species have also documented the possible activation of the hypothalamo-hypophyseal system, particularly in relation to the secretion of that exogenous testosterone may have either pro- or anti-gonadal effect depending upon the sexual status of the bird (Tewary *et al.*, 1985).

Changing levels of thyroid hormones may also play an important role in determining the type and extent of the effects of the testosterone on neuroendocrine-gonadal axis from the late quiescent phase to the reproductive phase of annual reproductive cycle. In seasonal breeder, reproductive window is too small and therefore, the animal needs to have an internal regulation. The advantage of having a testosterone-dependent mechanism is that an "avoidable activity" is slowed down, stopped or postponed only for the period when it is actually needed. Testosterone species, the absence of an influence during regressive and quiescent phase on testis by a high or a low dose of testosterone suggests that the neuroendocrine-gonadal axis was inactive and the levels were not high enough to act directly at the germinal epithelium (Thapliyal and Singh, 1995).

The results are shown in figure 10.1a. The mean body mass was slightly increased among all the three groups and The testis volume of group 2 and 3 received 50µg and 100µg TP respectively was significantly stimulated under SDLS and then transferred to LDL for next 30 days then the testis volume of 100µg TP group was more significantly stimulated. At low doses, circulating levels of testosterone remain normal or below normal and, therefore, TP produces an antigonadal response by the negative feedback actions on the hypothalamo-hypophyseal (h-h) system (Stetson, 1972). But, once the circulating levels become sufficiently higher after administration of high doses, TP directly acts on the seminiferous tubules leading to stimulation and/or maintenance of the growth of the regressed testes (Desjardins and Turek, 1977).

REFERENCES

Ashley, N.T., Hays, Q.R., Bentley, G.E. and Wingfield, J.C. 2009. Testosterone Treatment Diminishes Sickness Behaviour in Male Songbirds. *Horm Behav.* 56: 169-76.

Bentley, G.E., Ubuka, T., Mcguire, N.L., Calisi, R., Perfito, N., Kriegsfeld, L.J., Wingfield, J.C. and Tsutsui, K. 2009. Gonadotropin-inhibitory Hormone: A Multifunctional Neuropeptide. *J. Neuroendocrinol.* 21: 276-81.

Bridge, E.S., Schoech, S.J., Bowman, R. and Wingfield, J.C. 2009. Temporal Periodicity in Food Availability: Effects upon the Reproductive Axis in Scrub-Jays. *J. Exp. Zoo.* 311: 35-44.

Brown, N.L. and Follett, B.K. 1977. Effect of androgen on the Testes of Intact and hypophysectomized Japanese Quail. *Gen. Comp. Endocrinol.* 33: 267-277.

Davies, D.T. and Bicknell, R.J. 1976. The Effect of Testosterone on the Responsiveness of the Quail's Pituitary to Luteinizing Hormone-releasing Hormone (LH-RH) during Photoperiodically Induced Testicular Growth. *Gen. Comp. Endocrinol.* 30: 487-499.

Desjardins, C. and Turek, F.W. 1977. Effects of Testosterone on Spermatogenesis and Luteinizing Hormone Release in Japanese Quail. *Gen. Comp. Endocrinol.* 33: 293-303.

Farner, D.S., Donham, R.S., Matt, K.S., Mattocks, P.W., Moore, M.C. and Wingfield, J.C. 1983. The Nature of Photorefractoriness. In: Mikami S, Homma K, Wada M, Editors. Avian Endocrinology, Environmental and Ecological Perspective. *Japan Sci. Soc. Press.* Tokyo, Springer-Verlag. 149-166.

Hirschenhauser, K., Winkler, H. and Oliveria, R.F. 2003. Comparative Analysis of Male Androgen Responsiveness to Social Environment in Birds: The Effects of Mating System and Paternal Incubation. *Horm. Behav.* 43: 508-519.

Kumar, A., 2013. Role of Photoperiodic Responses on Body Weight and Testes in Brahminy Myna. *Journal of Scientific and Applied Research,* 4(1): 18-21.

Kumar, P., Pati, A.K., Mohan, J., Sastry, K.V.H., Tyagi, J.S. and Chaturvedi, C.M. 2009. Effect of Simulated Hypo- and Hyper-reproductive Conditions on the Characteristics of Circadian Rhythm in Hypothalamic Concentration of Serotonin and Dopamine and in Plasma Levels of Thyroxine, Triidothyronine, and Testosterone in Japanese Quail, *Coturnix coturnix japonica. Chronobiology International.* 26: 28-46.

Kumar, V. and Kumar, B.S. 1990. Effects of Photoperiod, Gonadactomy and Testosterone Therapy on Food intake and Body Weight in Male Redheaded Bunting, *Embriza bruniceps. J. Repod. Biol. Comp. Endocrinol.* 2: 80-87.

Kumaran, J.D.S and Turner, C.W. 1949. The Endocrinology of Spermatogenesis in Birds. II Effect of Androgens. *Pout. Sci.* 28: 739-746.

Lofts, B. 1962. Photoperiod and the Refractory Period of Reproduction in the Equatorial Bird *(Quelea quelea). Ibis.* 104: 407-414.

Pandey, R.K. and Bhardwaj S.K. (2015). Photoperiodic Regulation of Seasonal Responses in Indian Weaver Bird (*Ploceus philippinus*). *Biol. Rhythm Res.,* 46 (4): 483-495.

Sharma, D.K., Arvind, K. and Kumar, B.S. 2007. Influence of Testosterone on Body Mass and Testicular Response in the Brahminy Myna (*Sturnus pagodarum*). *Proceeding of RAAZ,* C.C.S. University Meerut, India.

Stetson, M.H. 1972. *Control Mechanisms in Avian Hypothalamo-hypophyseal-gonadal axis.* Ph.D. Thesis. University of Washington, Seattle.

Tewary, P.D., Tripathi, P.M. and Tripathi, B.K. 1985. Effects of Exogenous Gonadal Steroids and Castration of Photoperiodic Responses of the Yellow-throated Sparrow. *Indian J. Exp. Bio.* 23: 426-428.

Thapliyal, J.P. and Singh, V.K. 1995. Role of Male Hormone in the Regulation of the Annual Body Weight and Gonad Development Cycles of Migratory Male Redheaded Bunting, *Embriza Bruniceps. Pavo*. 33: 63-92.

Turek, F.W., McMillan, J.P. and Menaker, M. 1976. Melatonin: Effects on the Circadian Locomotor Rhythm in Sparrows. *Science*. 194: 1441-1443.

Wingfield, J.C. and Farner, D.S. 1993. Endocrinology of Reproduction in Wild Species. In: *Avian Biology*, Vol. IX. Academic Press. 163-277.

Pages: 107-116

Renewable Resources and Environment
Edited by: Dr. Baby Tabassum
ISBN: 978-93-5056-893-4
Edition: 2018
Published by: Discovery Publishing House Pvt. Ltd., New Delhi (India)

Agrochemicals and Soil Degradation

Nisha Verma

India is an agricultural country. About seventy percent of our population depends on agriculture. One-third of our National income comes from agriculture. Our economy is based on agriculture. The development of agriculture has much to do with the economic welfare of our country. There are two main crop seasons, namely kharif (May-October) and rabi (October-April). The major kharif crops include paddy, sorghum, pearl millet, maize, cotton, sugar cane, soybean and groundnut, and the rabi crops are wheat, barley, gram, linseed, rapeseed and mustard. With its good range of climates and soils, India has a good potential for growing a wide range of horticultural crops such as fruits, vegetables, potato, tropical tuber crops, mushrooms, ornamental crops, medicinal and aromatic crops, spices and plantation crops. Food grain (cereals and pulses) crops dominant over all cultivation. The country has a diverse landscape and a climate varying from the areas with highest rainfall such as Mawsynram near Cherrapunji (Meghalaya) to the driest parts of western Rajasthan with negligible rain and from a hot and humid southern peninsula to the snow bound Himalayan Mountains. The climate of India has four seasons: winter (January-February), a hot summer (March-May), rainy

Department of Botany, Govt. P.G. College, Bilaspur, Rampur (U.P.) (India)
email: nisha6oct@rediffmail.com

southwest monsoon (June-September), and post-monsoon (October-December). In India there is great diversity in landforms and climate conditions, all the major soils of the world are represented in India. Indian soils consist of eight major groups, out of which four are of agricultural importance, alluvial soils, black soils, red soils and lateritic soils. The four other soil groups that occur extensively in India are saline and sodic soils, desert soils, forest and hill soils and peaty and marshy soils.

1. **Alluvial soils:** Alluvial soils constitute the largest and most fertile soil group of India and contribute most to the agricultural wealth of the country. The soils are derived from the deposition of silt by the numerous rivers in plains, valleys and deltas. Alluvial soil found in the Assam valley, Western plains, Gujarat Plains, Indo-Gangetic Plains, Brahmaputra Valley and in the states of Punjab, Haryana, Uttaranchal, Uttar Pradesh, Bihar, West Bengal, Assam and the coastal regions of India. These soils are deficient in nitrogen, phosphorus and organic matter. Color of alluvial soil differ from the light grey to ash grey. Alluvial soils are very important for the growth of the various crops like cereals and pulses.
2. **Black soils:** These soils are also known as Regur soils or Black cotton soils. The Black soil is formed by solidification of lava spread over large area of deccan plateau. These soils are found in Karnataka, Maharashtra, MP, Gujarat, AP and Tamil Nadu. Black soils are generally clayey, deep and impermeable, these soils has the capacity to retain moisture for the longer duration compare to other soils, when moisture and water evaporated then soils develop cracks. Black soils are very rich in minerals contents because these soils were formed due to volcanic activities. These soils contains high quantities of Iron, Aluminium, Magnesium and lime, however they are poor in organic matter, Nitrogen and Phosphorous. Under rain fed conditions, they are used for growing cotton, millets, soybean, sorghum, pigeon

pea, etc. Under irrigated conditions, they can be used for a variety of other crops, such as sugar cane, wheat, tobacco and citrus crops

3. **Red Soils:** Ancient crystalline and metamorphic rocks have given rise to red soils.The soils are reddish in color because presence of iron oxide in it. These soils are found in the states of Andhra Pradesh, Tamil Nadu, Karnataka, Maharashtra, Orissa, Goa and in the northeastern states. They have limitations of soil depth, poor water and nutrient-holding capacity, excessive drainage, runoff and are generally poor in Nitrogen, Phosphorous, Zinc, Sulphur and humus.They are mainly used for cultivation of millets, rice, groundnut, maize, soybean, pigeon pea, green gram, jute, tea, cashew, cocoa, grapes, banana, papaya and mango.
4. **Laterite Soils:** Laterite soils are deeply weathered soils with a high clay content. These soils are formed due to coming of dry and wet seasons alternately. The soils mainly found in those areas where rainfall occur more than 200 cm. More rainfall causes leaching away of laterite rocks because of which parts of silica and lime go down and Iron and Aluminium are left in form of soil. The soils include deficiency of Phosphorous, Potassium, Calcium, Zinc and Boron. They are generally found in Kerala, Tamil Nadu, Karnataka, Andhra Pradesh and some part of Orissa. The important crops grown on these soils are rice, banana, coconut, areca nut, cocoa, cashew, coffee, tea and rubber.
5. **Arid or Desert soils:** Desert soils constitute the sandy soil with negligible vegetation. It is water deficient soil. The color of these soils range from Red to Brown. These soils are rich in Phosphorous and Iron but deficient in humus and Nitrogen. These are infertile soils which are alkaline in nature. These soils are very prone to wind erosion. Coarse cereals like jowar, bajara and ragi are cultivated in this soils. This soil is found in extremely arid areas such as Bikaner and Jaisalmer in Rajasthan.

6. **Saline and Alkaline Soils:** These soils are also called Reh, Usar, or Kallar. The saline soils also contain higher proportion of Sodium, Potassium and Magnesium and lack in Nitrogen and Calcium. They are widely distributed in Western Gujarat, Eastern coast deltas, Sunder bans areas and in Rajasthan and Maharashtra. The soil has poor physical conditions and nutrient deficiency. By using gypsum soil is used successfully for growing rice and wheat. In coastal areas coconut trees are found plenty in these soils.
7. **Mountains and Forest Soils:** Mountain soils are found at high as well as low elevations where rainfall is sufficiently high. Soil formation is governed mainly by the deposition of organic matter derived from the forest growth. Soils are found in himalayan areas. These soils are rich in fossils but they are under composed so humic acid formed and soils became acidic. These soils are poor in Potash, Phosphorus and Lime. These soils are affected by problem of soil erosion. Tea, Coffee and fruits are grown in these soils.
8. **Peaty and Marshy soils:** Peaty and marshy soils are formed by plants growing in the humid regions under permanently waterlogged conditions. They are found in Kerala, Orissa, West Bengal (Sundarbans) and along the South-East coast of Tamil Nadu. These soils are found in those areas where high amount of rainfall occur. They have good growth of vegetation and are rich in humus and organic matter. Peaty soils are heavy and brown in color......Soil is a complex structure and contains five major components i.e. mineral matter, water, air, organic matter and living organisms. The quantity of these components in the soil does not remain the same but varies with the locality. Soil possesses not only a nucleus position for existence of living being but also ensures their future existence. Soil serves many vital functions in our society, particularly for food production. It is essential to make an adequate land management to

maintain the quality of soil in both rural and urban areas. Soil is a fundamental resource base for agricultural production systems. Besides being the main medium for plant growth, soil functions to sustain plant productivity, maintain environmental quality and provide nutrition for plant, animal and human health. Until the industrial revolution of the early to mid-1900's, agriculture practices were environmentally friendly. Crop yields in agricultural systems depended on internal resources, recycling of organic matter and rainfall patterns. Formers used crop rotation to maintain soil nutrients and involved little or no heavy machinery. In these types of farming systems the link between agriculture and ecology was quite strong. But as agricultural modernization progressed, the ecology-farming linkage was often broken. The modernization of farming practices resulted in extreme increases in productivity but there is the degradation of environmental quality. Modern agricultural practices use intensive tillage, monoculture, irrigation, application of inorganic fertilizers, chemical pest control and plant genome modification to maximize profit and production. These practices greatly increased crop yields. However, on these practices have led to soil degradation which is one of the most serious consequences of conventional agriculture.

Soil is subject to a series of degradation processes. Soil can be degraded by salting, water logging, compaction, pesticide contamination, decline in soil structure quality, loss of fertility, erosion, lowering of the water table, overcutting of vegetation, shifting cultivation, overgrazing., non-adoption of soil-conservation management practices, extension of cultivation, improper crop rotations, unbalanced fertilizer use and over pumping of groundwater.

Soil degradation may be of three type, Physical degradation, Chemical degradation and Biological degradation. Physical degradation is caused when agricultural practices impact the physical property of soils. Use of heavy farm machinery reduce capacity of soils to retain and supply water and air to growing plants. Chemical degradation caused by inappropriate use of Fertilizers and Pesticides. Prolonged use of heavy doses of fertilizers can result in soils becoming more acidic that has serious implications in terms of long term productivity of soils. Pest control chemicals utilised to eliminate unwanted pests are also destroyed the living soil organisms. These soil organisms are necessary for soil health and productivity. Biological degradation causes depletion of organic matter and reduced biodiversity. Soils are a habitat to a large variety of flora and fauna that constitute a significant part of our biodiversity resource. Organic matter is the main food base of living organisms in the soil and soil organisms perform vital functions that contribute to sustained productivity of soils. Reduced recycling of organics through the soil is the primary factor leading to a decline in the extent and diversity of living organisms within it.

Soil quality describe the combination of chemical, physical and biological characteristics that enables soil to perform a wide range of functions. Soil health and soil quality are terms used interchangeably to describe soils that are not only fertile but also possess adequate physical and biological properties to sustain productivity, maintain environmental quality and promote plant. Soil fertility is only one component of soil quality. Fertile soils are able to provide the nutrients required for plant growth, these are the chemical components of soil. Soil contamination or soil pollution is caused by the presence of man-made chemicals. Agricultural chemicals, industrial activity or improper disposal of wastes typically causes it.

Agrochemicals are used in agricultural to ensure an abundant food supply. Many important benefits are achieved by the use of agrochemicals. These are largely associated with increased yields of plant and animal crops and less spoilage during storage. However, the use of certain agrochemicals has also been associated environmental and ecological damages. Extensive use of these agrochemicals leads to soil quality degradation. Pesticides, which are very persistent in soil, slowly break down and result in source of contamination. Soil acts as filter, buffer and degradation potentials with respect to storage of pollutant. Soil is a potential pathway of pesticide transport to contaminate water, air, plants, food and ultimately to human. Inappropriate use of chemical fertilizers and pesticides, amongst common farming practices, can contribute significantly to the soil degradation process. Imbalanced or excessive, use of fertilizers is a major cause of pollution of ground waters or surface water bodies. Many of the chemicals used in pesticides are persistent soil contaminants, whose impact may endure for decades and adversely affect soil conservation. Pesticides enter the soil via spray drift during foliage treatment, wash-off from treated foliage, release from granulates or from treated seeds in soil. The presence of pesticides in soil can adversely impact human and animal health. These are detrimental to living organisms in the soil, vital to soil health and productivity. Pesticides can move off-site contaminating surface and groundwater and possibly causing adverse impacts on aquatic ecosystems. Among organic pollutants some are referred to as persistent organic pollutants, which do not break down quickly in the environment and persist for a longer period thereby resulting to various hazardous consequences. Continuous and excessive use of pesticide compounds has led to the contamination of ecosystems. The pollution of heavy metals poses a threat to a country's food production. Some fertilizers and pesticides are known to contain various levels of heavy metals, including Cd and Cu. Therefore, continuous and heavy application of these agrochemicals and other soil amendments can potentially exacerbate the accumulation of heavy metals in agricultural soils over time.

Soil microorganisms play a key role in soil. They are essential for maintenance of soil structure, transformation and mineralization of organic matter, making nutrients available for plants. External agricultural inputs such as mineral fertilizers, organic amendments, microbial inoculants, and pesticides are applied with the ultimate goal of maximizing productivity and economic returns, while side effects on soil organisms are often neglected.

The excessive agrochemicals application reduces the biodiversity of the soil microorganisms. The microorganisms of soil are more spoiled by application of chemicals than any other parameters. The communities of beneficial microorganisms in soil have declined due to overuse of pesticides, which has a negative impact on the available nitrogen, phosphorus and potassium from soil, thereby degrading the soil quality. Important processes like mineralization, nitrification and phosphorus recycling are dependent much on the balanced equilibrium existing among various groups of organisms in the soil. However, extensive pesticide usage disturbs the presence of soil enzymes.

The primary impact of soil degradation is a substantial reduction in the productivity of soil and land directly impacting those whose livelihoods depend on this natural resource. Soil degradation processes are generally insidious and show up only gradually as the problem becomes more and more severe. Reduced ability of soils to absorb rain water would imply increased runoff and erosion causing adverse downstream impact including filling up of water bodies, aquatic life etc. Soil degradation processes cause reduced aboveground and underground biodiversity, decline in water quality and overall ecosystem health. In the initial stages the farmers tend to compensate for the yield loss on account of soil degradation by resorting to applying more fertilizer thereby increasing cultivation costs. Impact of soil degradation processes often extends beyond direct yield losses and in extreme cases the soils can turn unfit for agriculture, seriously affecting a farmer's ability to sustain livelihoods. Unfortunately, industrial agriculture practices continue to damage and deplete this valuable natural resource. While intensive plowing and monocrop agriculture systems have caused nutrient depletion and wide-scale soil erosion, over-application of fertilizers and pesticides has contaminated our soils and polluted our waterways. Fortunately, many farmers are choosing to use sustainable agricultural techniques such as conservation tillage, crop rotation, and organic fertilization in order to protect our valuable soil resources. They are aware of and already fertilizing soils and protecting crops with organic and sustainable techniques that work with nature, not against it, and can provide food for all.

REFERENCES

Abrahams, P.W.(2002) *Soils: their Implications to Human Health*, Sci. Total Environ., 291, 1-32.

Burauel, P.; Bassmann, F. (2005) *Soils as Filter and Buffer for Pesticides: Experimental Concepts to Understand Soil Functions*, Environ. Pollut., 133, 11-6.

Doran, J.W. (1994) *Defining Soil Quality for a Sustainable Environment*. Madison, Wis.: Soil Science Society of America.

Eijsackers, H.; Beneke, P.; Maboeta, M.; Louw, J.; Reinecke, A.; (2005) *The Implications of Copper Fungicide Usage in Vineyards for Earthworm Activity and Resulting Sustainable Soil Quality*. Ecotoxicology and Environmental Safety 62, 2005, 99-111.

Gliessman, S.R. (1998) *Agroecology: Ecological Processes in Sustainable Agriculture*. Ann Arbor Press, Chelsea, MI.

Kabata-Pendias, A.; Pendias, H.(1992) *Trace Elements in Soils and Plants*, 2nd. CRC Press, Boca Raton, FL.

Karishma Baishya. (2015) *Impact of Agrochemicals Application on Soil Quality Degradation*. IJSTM. Vol. No. 04.

Lal, R. (2002) *Soil Carbon Dynamics in Cropland and Rangeland*. Environmental Pollution, 116, 353-362.

Loureiro, S.; Soares, A.M.V.M.; Nogueira, A.J.A. (2005) *Terrestrial Avoidance Behaviour Tests as Screening Tool to Assess Soil Contamination*. Environmental Pollution 138, 121-131.

Merrington, G.; Rogers, S.L.; Zwieten, L.V. (2002) *The Potential Impact of Long-term Copper Fungicide Usage on Soil Microbial Biomass and Microbial Activity in an Avocado Orchard*. Australian Journal of Soil Research 40, 749-759.

Nawab, A.; Aleem, A.; Malik, A. (2003) *Determination of Organochlorine Pesticides in Agricultural Soil with Special Reference to ã-HCH Degradation by Pseudomonas Strains*. Bioresource Technol., 88, 41-46.

Pandey, S.; Singh, D.K. (2004) *Total Bacterial and Fungal Population after Chlorpyrifos and Quinalphos Treatments in Groundnut (Arachis hypogaea L.) Soil*. Chemosphere 55, 197-205.

Sardar, D.; Kole, R.K. (2005) *Metabolism of Chlorpyrifos in Relation to its Effect on the Availability of some Plant Nutrients in Soil,Chemosphere,* 61: 1273-1280.

Siamwalla, A. (1996) *Agricultural Sustainability in Rapidly Industrializing Asian Economies. In: Integration of Sustainable Agriculture and Rural Development in Agricultural Policy,* FAO/Winrock International.

Singh, J. Singh, D.K. (2005) *Dehydrogenase and Phosphomonoesterase Activities in Groundnut (Arachis hypogaea L.) Field after Diazinon, Imidacloprid and Lindane Treatments.* Chemosphere 60, 32-42.

Singh, R.B. (2000) *Environmental Consequences of Agricultural Development: A Case Study from the Green Revolution State of Haryana, India, Agriculture, Ecosystems and Environment,* Vol. 82 No. 1-3, 97-103.

Stephenson, G.A.; Solomon, K.R. (1993) *Pesticides and the Environment.* Department of Environmental Biology, University of Guelph, Guelph, Ontario, Canada.

Zhang, H.B.; Luo, Y.M.; Zhao, Q.G. (2006) *Residues of Organochlorine Pesticides in Hong Kong Soils,* Chemo-sphere, 63, 633-641.

Pages: 117-123

Renewable Resources and Environment
***Edited by:* Dr. Baby Tabassum**
ISBN: 978-93-5056-893-4
***Edition:* 2018**
***Published by:* Discovery Publishing House Pvt. Ltd., New Delhi (India)**

Brief Review Article on the Pharmacological Activities of *Azadirachta Indica* (Neem)

Baby Tabassum; Priya Bajaj and Robeer.a Sarah

ABSTRACT

The paper reviews the pharmaceutical and clinical importance of neem. Neem is a natural resource to keep the environment clean and healthy. Every part of Neem tree is beneficial for human use. Neem tree offers the World a wide variety of medicines, pesticides, cosmetics, and fertilizers and helps to solve challenging problems like pollution, epidemics and infectious diseases. Neem gives out more oxygen than other trees. Since the last few years neem is getting extraordinary popularity across the world. It is called a 'domestic doctor' in India due to its common availability and wide efficacy. The role of neem tree in controlling water, air and land pollution is wonderful. It possesses a number of pharmacological activities. The seeds, barks and leaves contain compounds with proven antiseptic, antiviral, antipyretic, anti-inflammatory, anti-fungal and anti-ulcer uses. It is widespread and is cheaper, easily accessible. There are some 14 million neem trees in India. Neem tree is the most researched tree in the World and is said to be the most promising tree of 21st century.

Toxicology Laboratory, Department of Zoology, Govt. Raza P.G. College, Rampur (U.P.) (India)

INTRODUCTION

Nature has been a source of medicinal agents for thousands of years and an impressive number of modern drugs have been isolated from them, many based on their use in traditional medicine. Sixty per cent of the world population and 80% of the population in developing countries rely on traditional medicine for curing many diseases. The natural products form an integral part of human life from ancient civilizations to the current century and more than half of the drugs in the market are natural products or derivatives of them. Medicinal plants play a significant role in modern medicine.

Neem (*Azadirachta indica*) is one of the most popular, auspicious and well-known trees which is more extensively studied for its pharmaceutical and clinical properties. It is a tropical evergreen tree native to India and is also found in other southeast countries. It is commonly called 'Indian lilac' or 'Margosa' and belongs to the family Meliaceae. The Persian name of neem is *'Azad- Darakth- E- Hind'* which means 'Free tree of India'. Neem is a natural resource to keep the environment clean and healthy. Every part of Neem tree is beneficial for human use. Neem tree offers the World a wide variety of medicines, pesticides, cosmetics, and fertilizers and help solve challenging problems like pollution, epidemics and infectious diseases. Neem have been known to possess a wide range of pharmacological properties, especially as antibacterial, antifungal, antiulcer, antifeedant, repellent, pesticide, inhibitor and sterilant. Neem grows on almost any kind of soil and requires little water. It grows best in black soil and has a widespread natural distribution. These trees have a life of 200 yrs. and grow up to altitude of 3000 ft.

In the last 70 years, there has been a lot of research on the pharmacological properties of neem, conducted in various esteemed institutes of India. A number of commercial products of neem like pesticides, cosmetics, medicines etc. came in the market in recent years. Neem is also called as 'Village Pharmacy' and is considered in the Ancient Indian History to be of divine origin. It is widespread and is cheaper, easily accessible. There are some 14 million neem trees in India and the age-old techniques for extracting the oil does not require expensive equipments. Neem gives out more oxygen than other trees. In Uttar Pradesh, village surrounded with neem trees, were frequently considered as Free from Ailments.

TAXONOMIC CLASSIFICATION & CHEMICAL COMPONENTS OF *A. INDICA*

The neem tree has been described as *A. indica* as early as 1830 by De Jussieu and its taxonomic position is as follows:

Order	Rutales
Suborder	Rutinae
Family Meliaceae	(mahogany family)
Subfamily	Melioideae
Tribe	Melieae
Genus	*Azadirachta*
Species	*indica*

Four major (high percentage) compounds were identified in *A. indica* is n- hexadecanoic acid (14.34%), phytol (19.96%), 9, 12, 15- octa- decatrienoic acid, (18.57%), and vitamin E (11.37%). Neem contains at least 35 biologically active principles of which nimbin and azadirachtin are the most active ingredients and are present mostly in the seeds, leaves and other parts of the neem. The extracts are beneficial for heart diseases, hepatitis, fungal infection, malaria, psoriasis, and ulcers.

MEDICINAL USE OF VARIOUS PARTS OF NEEM

There are several reports on the biological activities and pharmacological actions of neem based on modern scientific investigations. Biological activity of neem is reported with the crude extracts and their different fractions from leaf, bark, root, seed and oil. However, crude extract of different parts of neem have been used as traditional medicine for the treatment of various diseases.

Table 12.1

Some medicinal uses of neem as mentioned in ayurveda (Biswas, 2002)

Part	Medicinal use
Leaf	Leprosy, eye problem, epistaxis, intestinal worms, anorexia, biliousness, skin ulcers.
Bark	Analgesic, alternative and curative of fever.
Flower	Bile suppression, elimination of intestinal worms and phlegm.
Fruit	Relieves piles, intestinal worms, urinary disorder, epistaxis, phlegm, eye problem, diabetes, wounds and leprosy.
Twig	Relieves cough, asthma, piles, phantom tumour, intestinal worms, spermatorrhoea, obstinate urinary disorder, diabetes.
Gum	Effective against skin diseases like ringworms, scabies, wounds and ulcers.
Seed pulp	Leprosy and intestinal worms.
Oil	Leprosy and intestinal worms.
Root, bark, leaf, flower and fruit together	Blood morbidity, biliary afflictions, itching, skin ulcer, burning sensation and leprosy.

PHARMACOLOGICAL ACTIVITIES OF *A. INDICA*

Almost every part of Neem tree has been known to possess a wide range of pharmacological properties (Biswas *et.al.*, 2002). Some of them are as follows:

1. **Neem twigs (datun) as Toothbrush:** Many of India's 80% rural population still start their day with the chewing stick, while in urban areas neem toothpaste is preferred. It has been found to be as effective as a toothbrush in reducing plaque and gingival inflammation.
2. **Neem in Cosmetics:** Recently the awareness regarding the adverse effects of chemical cosmetics has raised a demand for cosmetics made from natural products which are safe for human skin and body. Neem is being used almost in every kind of cosmetic product. It is used as a main ingredient in soaps, shampoos, moisturizers, creams, tooth pastes, talcum powders etc.

3. **As Pesticide and Fertilizers:** The adverse effect of chemical fertilizers and pesticides on human health has brought a need for organic fertilizers and pesticide, which are environmentally safe, good for health, cheaper and easy to use. Neem is one of the primary herbs used as an organic fertilizer and pesticide in most parts of the world. Neem oil mixed with kerosene is used as a pesticide. 'Nimbin', an organic pesticide is obtained from Neem cake. Neem extract is used as a pesticide and Neem oil is used as bug repellant. Azardirachtin, the active compound from the seeds of Neem is the main component responsible for the anti feedant and toxic effects in insects.
4. **For controlling Blood Glucose:** Diabetes is one of the most prevalent disease in most parts of the world and is epidemic now. Conventional medicine is good for controlling diabetes but not for curing it. Intake of Neem leaves and its extract has been proved to be beneficial for not only keeping blood sugar under control but also curing the disease.
5. **Hepatoprotective role of neem:** Co-administration of *Azadirachta indica* leaf extract with arsenic to rats, effectively reduced the extent of liver damage as levels of serum enzymes and hepatic anti-oxidants were modulated close to normal. (Oyewole, 2011).
6. **For improving Water Quality and health of Fish:** Neem Leave Powder (NLP) efficiently remove cadmium from water decreasing it in tissues of fish while Neem Leave Water Extract (NLWE) removes cadmium in low degree but affect significantly the haematological, physiological and immunological state of *O. niloticus*, improving health status of fish (Osman and Hegazy, 2013).
7. **Role of Neem in controlling Environmental Pollution:** Medicinal plants have an important role to play in protecting our environment too. As the leaf canopy of neem tree is so thick it is an excellent source of oxygen. It is a wonder tree and can be used to prevent disease,

epidemics, pollution and saving the environment. The role of neem tree in controlling water, air and land pollution is wonderful. Neem is a natural resource to keep the environment clean and healthy.

8. **As Mosquito Repellant:** The biological activity of neem extract might be due to active compounds in Neem including phenolics, terpenoids, & alkaloids which may also lead to death of mosquitoes.

CONCLUSION

Medicinal plants can be used not only as remedy but even as growth promoters, stress resistance boosters and preventatives of infections. Thus, the medicinal plants in disease management are gaining success, because they are cheaper and exhibit no or very less toxicity. They are rich in a wide variety of phytochemicals, *e.g.*, tannins, alkaloids and flavonoids, which act against several diseases (Pandey and Madhuri, 2010). Neem has a long history as a medicinal plant with diverse therapeutic uses. It is considered to be a part of India's genetic diversity. Neem tree is the most researched tree in the world and is said to be the most promising tree of 21st century. With the advancement of technologies, it has become easier to extract and characterize the active compounds of neem. It has great potential in the fields of pest management, environment protection and medicine. Neem is a natural source of insecticides, pesticides and agrochemicals (Girish, 2008). Therefore, it is also called as 'Village Pharmacy' and is considered in the Ancient Indian History to be of divine origin.

REFERENCES

Biswas, K. *et.al.*, (2002): Biological Activities and Medicinal Properties of Neem (*Azadirachta indica*). Current Science. Vol. 82 (11).

De Jussieu, A., *Mem. Mus. Hist. Nat., Paris*, 1830, 19, 220.

Girish K. *et al*; Neem – A Green Treasure *Electronic Journal of Biology*, 2008, Vol. 4(3): 102-111.

Oyewole, I.O., (2011): Ameliorating Effect of Methanolic Leaf Extract of *Azadirachta indica* (neem) on Arsenic-induced Oxidative Damage in Rat liver. Int. J. of Toxicol. & Applied Pharmacology.

Osman, H.A.M. and Hegazy A.M. (2013): Removal of Cadmium from Fresh Water Cultured Nile tilapia Oreochromis niloticus using Neem Leave Water Extract (NLWE) and Neem Leave Powder (NLP). Nature and Science. 11(12).

Pandey, Govind and S. Madhuri (2010). Significance of Fruits and Vegetables in Malnutrition Cancer. *Pl. Arch.,* 10(2): 517-522.

Pages: 124-133

Renewable Resources and Environment
Edited by: Dr. Baby Tabassum
ISBN: 978-93-5056-893-4
Edition: 2018
Published by: Discovery Publishing House Pvt. Ltd., New Delhi (India)

Impact of Malathion on Oxygen Consumption in an Air Breathing Fish *Channa Gachua*

Qaisur Rahman[1] and Baby Tabassum[2]

ABSTRACT

Pesticides belong to important class of chemicals that pose continuous liability to the stability of aquatic ecosystem. Indiscriminate excessive and injudicious use of pesticides has resulted in pollution of general environment including water, air, soil and food. Water pollution by pesticides is a serious problem for aquatic flora, fauna and for us as fishes form important source of food for human beings. Pesticides are known to enter into the rivers and streams mainly through the aerial sprays operated to control the pests in forests and agricultural areas. Another source of entry of pesticides is rain water. In the present study an attempt has been made to study impact of malathion on oxygen consumption of fresh water fish *Channa gachua*. The fishes were exposed to 96 hours sub lethal concentration (0.8 ppm). The period of exposure was 24 hours, 48 hours, 72 hours and 96 hours for sub lethal concentration. The result indicates that the rate of oxygen consumption decreased in 24-92 hours in sub lethal concentration compared with control. Present study showed

1 Dept. of Zoology, Vinoba Bhave University, Hazaribagh, Pin - 825 301 (Jharkhand) (India)

2 Dept. of Zoology, Govt Raza, Post Graduate College, Rampur, Pin - 244 901 (U.P.) (India)

email: qaisur.rahman@gmail.com

that malathion altered respiratory metabolism in *Channa gachua* which can used as bio-indicator for assessing pesticide toxicity to fish.The details will be discussed in this paper.

Keywords: Malathion, Oxygen consumption, *Channa gachua*.

INTRODUCTION

The pollution of rivers and streams with chemical contaminant has become one of the most critical environmental problems of the centuries. Pesticides used in agricultural are one of the major source of water pollution. Such chemical may reach lakes and rivers through rains and wind and may affect non target organisms including fishes. Organo-phosphates have become the most widely used class of insecticide in the world replacing persistent problematic organochlorine compounds. Exposure of aquatic ecosystem to these insecticides is difficult to assess because of their short persistent in water column due to low solubility and rapid degradation hence monitoring of these insecticides is important Chebbi and David (2010) and Qaisur (2011) respectively. Since malathion is a non-systemic wide spectrum organophosphate insecticide. It was one of the earliest organophosphate insecticides developed in (1950). It is widely used organophosphate insecticide because of its relatively low toxicity to mammals and high selectivity for insects compared with other organophosphate insecticides. There are many earlier finding that clearly warned of the genotoxic potential of technical grade malathion in wide range of organisms including fish (Kushwaha *et al.,* 2000). Once malathion is introduced into the environment usually from spraying on crops or in wide urban or residential areas, it may cause problems to aquatic organisms including fishes. In watermalathion breaks down quickly by the action of water and bacteria in the water. Qaisur and Sadhu (2009) reported that change in respiratory rate is one of the common physiological responses to toxicant including pesticide and easily detectable through changes in oxygen consumption rate which frequently used to evaluate the changes in metabolism under environmental conditions. This paper reveals the impact of sublethal concentration of malathion on oxygen consumption of fresh water fish *Channa gachua*.

MATERIALS AND METHODS

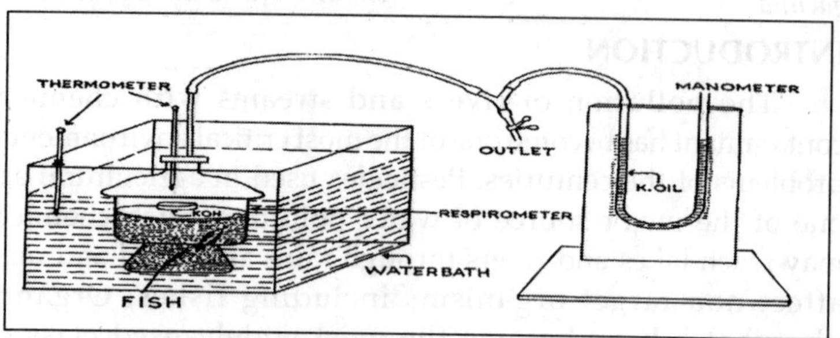

Fig. 13.1: Experimental set up for the measurements of dual mode of oxygen uptake in *Channa gchua*

Live specimens of *Channa gachua* were procured from local fish dealers at Hazaribag (Latitude 25° 59′N and Longitude 85° 22′E) and maintained in large glass aquaria size (90×60×60cm) with continuous flow of water. The fish were fed on chopped goat liver daily during a minimum acclimation period of 15 days in the laboratory. Routine oxygen consumption from air and still water was measured in a closed glass respirometer containing 3 litres of water (initial O_2 content = 6.5 mg O_2/Litre; pH = 7.2) and 0.51 ML of air (Fig. 13.1). The fish had free access to air through a small semi circular hole (10 cm diameter) in a disc float. Carbosorb (B.D.H) or KOH in a petridish placed on the float absorbed CO_2. Thus the fish could exchange gases with water by way of its gills as well as with the air using the suprabranchial chamber. The air phase of respirometer was connected to a differential manometer. Movement of the manometer fluid follow uptake of oxygen when the CO_2 is absorbed by Carbosorb (KOH). The fish were acclimatized to the respirometers at least 12 hours before the reading were taken. The concentration of dissolved oxygen in the water was estimated by Winklers Volumetric method (Welch, 1948). The oxygen uptake through gills was calculated from the difference between the oxygen levels of the ambient water in the respirometer before and after the experiment and the reading of volume of water in the respirometer. Oxygen uptake from air was measured and calculated the reading volume change in the manometer and by the use of the combined gas law equations and vapour pressure (Dejours, 1975). Mean values of oxygen consumption of a series of observations, on each fish at STPD and standard errors were calculated. The experiments were conducted at 29.0 ± 1.5°C. The pH of the ambient water was measured by an electronic pH meter (systronics). The respiratory chambers were thermostated by immersion in a temperature controlled water bath. The chamber was coated with black paint to avoid the activity of light.

Before starting the experiment fish *Channagachua*was left in running tap water for about 10 minute to facilitate them to reach a state of normality from a state of excitement if any. After this equilibrium period, one fish was kept in respiratory chamber without causing any damage to the animal and initial sample collected immediately. Then the fish was allowed to respire for one hour. Immediately after one hour final sample was collected. Rate of oxygen consumption were calculated considering net weight of fish. Two sets were carried out for normal and treated fish. In treated groups fishes were exposed to sublethal concentration of malathion (0.8) ppm which is 1/5th concentration of LC_{50} value. The total oxygen consumption and rate of oxygen consumption were measured at 24, 48, 72 and 96 hours. The values for total oxygen consumption were expressed as ml/kg/hr and rate of oxygen consumption was expressed as ml/kg/hr of fish tissue.

RESULTS

In present investigation total oxygen consumption was 2.37, 1.71, 0.85 and 0.76 ml/kg/hr of during 24, 48, 72 and 96 hours respectively in treated group. In control total oxygen consumption was 2.78 ml/kg/hr of oxygen consumption which indicate decreasing trend to compare with control ones.

The rate of oxygen consumption was 0.067, 0.048, 0.024 and 0.021 ml/kg/hr of *Channa gachua* weight of fish during 24, 48, 72 and 96 hours respectively which was reduced as compared with control. In control rate of oxygen consumption was 0.079 ml/kg/hr of oxygen consumption of fish. Hence oxygen consumption exhibited decreasing trend in treated group up to 96 hours as compared with control group.

Table 13.1

Showing oxygen consumption in *Channa gachua* exposed to Malathion

Sl. No.	Oxygen Consumption	Control	24 Hours	48 Hours	72 Hours	96 Hours
1.	Total oxygen consumption (ml/kg/hr)	2.78±0.38	2.37±0.18	1.71±0.12*	0.85±0.08*	0.76±0.16*
2	Rate of oxygen consumption (ml/kg/hr)	0.79±0.01	0.067±0.05*	0.048±0.003	0.024±0.002*	0.021±0.003*

Values are mean ± SD of ten replicates *p<0.05, **p< 0.01, ***p> 0.01, significant when student-t test was applied between control and experimental ones.

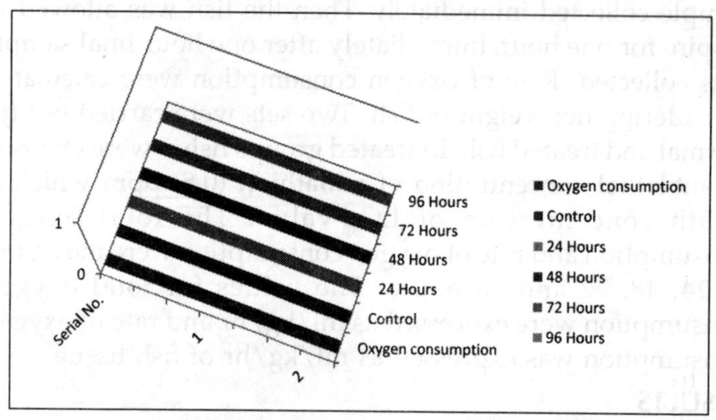

Graph 13.1: Showing oxygen consumption in *Channa gachua* at sublethal doses of Malathion

DISCUSSION

Most fish breathein the water in which they live changes in the chemical properties of water due to pesticide toxication reflected in the animal's ventilatory activity particularly affect respiratory gas exchange. Organophosphorus insecticides including malathion are widely used in crop protection. Indiscriminate application of these insecticides affects non-target organisms including economically important fresh water fish *Channa gachua*. A change in respiration rate is common physiological responses to toxicants. It is easily detectable through changes in oxygen consumption rate which frequently used to evaluate the changes in metabolism under environment deterioration. Many authors investigated that pesticide toxicity induced respiratory distress in fishes. David (2003) showed disturbances in oxidative metabolism in *Tilapia mossambica* under cypermethrin toxicity. Nataranjan (1981) showed reduction in oxygen consumption in *Channapunctatus* exposed to organophosphate pesticide. Boradbury *et al.*, (1986) stated that the greater decrease in the rate of oxygen consumption in the fish *Cirrhinusmrigala* may be due to internal action of pesticide as toxicant altering the metabolic cycle at subcellular level. Nagarathanamma and Ramamurty (1982) showed variation in the oxygen consumption of *Cyprinuscarpio* under methyl parathion stress. Khillare and Wagh (1987) observed reduced rate of oxygen consumption in the fish *Barbus stigma* when exposed to malathion and Nuvan respectively. Ali (1982) studied effect of pesticide, dimacron on fresh water fish, *Channapunctatus* and reported that respiration rate reduced in the fish. Lomte and Jadhav (1982) reported that decrease in oxygen consumption after pesticidal stress and observed in *Corbicularegularis*. Verma and Dalela (1975) showed that reduction in oxygen consumption of fish might be due to suspended solids present in the effluents which cause mechanical injuries to fish and disturb the osmotic regulation. Malla Reddy (1988) showed effect of fenvalerate and cypermethrin on the oxygen consumption of fish *Cyprinuscarpio* and reported significant drop in rate of oxygen consumption. Janardhan Rao (1991) studied oxygen consumption rate of *Macronussalki* exposed to endosulfan. He reported that oxygen consumption rates increased at 24 hours and decreased gradually at 48, 72 and 96 hours. Several authors reported that the disturbance in oxidative metabolism leads alteration in whole animal oxygen consumption in different species of fish exposed to pesticides (Holden, 1962; Ferguson and Good year, 1967; Wilkinson and Dension, 1982; David, 2003; Vatukuru, 2005; Vinnetkumar 2008; Anneta Susan, 2010) respectively.

The organophosphorus insecticide generally act as disruption of nerve impulses, transmission in the central and peripheral nervous system by inhibiting AChE, that hydrolyze the neurotransmitter, aceteylcholine (Aldridge, 1971; Fukuto, 1971; Brown, 1978). Inhibition of AChE by this pesticide group was reported to cause abnormalities in some of the vital physiological process like respiration and cardiovascular regulation (Eto, 1974; O'Brien, 1967; Corbeet, 1974; Murphy, 1980) respectively. In present investigation malathion was used to study its effect on respiratory metabolism of *Channagachua*. The result showed significant decrease in oxygen consumption and rate of oxygen consumption. Maheswari *et al.*, (2001) observed effect of triazophos to the fish *Clariusbatrachus* and reported that organophosphate was more toxic among other insecticide. Rao *et al.*, (2003) showed reduced oxygen consumption value of fish *Oreochromismossambicus* when exposed to organophosphorus pesticide chloropyrifos. Qaisur and Sadhu (2009) in *Channagachua* reported that the contamination of fish habitat by different pollutants is of great concern, sometimes causing heavy mortality of a localized fish population and their food organisms. Much information about the effect of environmental pollutants on aquatic animals has been obtained from mortality studies. Very little is known about the damage to different internal organs or processes within an organism following an exposure to environmental poisons. Consequently knowledge about the mode of action of toxicants and cause of death in poisoned aquatic animals is lacking. A better understanding of these mechanisms is necessary if we want to predict the potential harmfulness of various chemicals to these environments.Qaisur (2011) in

Channagachua reported that respiratory activity of a fish is often the first physiological response to be affected by the presence of contaminants in the aquatic environment. Although many biological early warning systems monitor abnormal opercular movement as an indicator of respiratory stress, a more direct measurement of stress in this sense necessitates the quantification of oxygen consumed by the fish. The oxygen consumption is not often used as a bioindicator of pollution associated stress in biological early warning systems. Respiratory responses were found to be less sensitive, but also could be successfully used in bioassay testing of treated industrial and municipal effluents before they are discharged into receiving waters. Gill ventilation frequency and coughing rate are intimately associated with respiratory demands and gill irritation or blockage. Oxygen consumption measurements provide a robust indicator of whole animal stress and concomitant water quality respectively.

REFERENCES

Aldridge W.N. 1971.The Nature of Reaction of Organophosphorus Compounds Carbamates with Esterases. *Bull. Cold. Hlth. Org.* 44: 120-126.

Ali S.M. 1982. Effect of Pesticides on Fresh Water Fishes Ph.D. Thesis Submitted to Marathwada University, Aurangabad, India.

Boradbury S.P., Cosasts J.R. and Mckim J. M. 1986.Toxicokineties of Fenvalerate in Rainbow Trout *Salmogairdeneri. Environ. Toxicol. Chem.* 5: 567-576.

Brown A.W.A. 1978. Ecology of Pesticides *In.* John Wiley Inter Sciences Publication. New York, Chickester, Brisbane, Toranto.

Chebbi S.G. and David M. 2010. Respiratory Responses and Behavioural Anomalies of the Carp *Cyprinuscarpio* under Qinalthos Intoxication in Sublethal Doses. *Sci. Asia.* 36: 12-17.

Corbeet J.R. (1974). In: The Biochemical mode of Pesticides, Academic Press, New York. N.Y. 165-186.

David M., Shivakumar H.B., Shivakumar R., Mushigeri S.B. and Ganthi B.H. 2003. Toxicity Evalution of Cypermethrin and its Effect on Oxygen Consumption of the Fresh Water Fish, *Tilapia mossambica. Indian. J. Envi. Toxicol.* 13: 99-102.

Dejour's P. 1975. "Principles of Comparative Respiratory Physiology." Amsterdum. North Holland Publishing Company pp. 253.

Eto, M. 1974. Organophosphorus Pesticides Organic and Biological Chemistry, CRC Press, Cleveland. 123-143 pp.

Ferguson D.E., Lude J.T., Murthy and G.G. 1967. Dynamics of Endrin uptake Release by Resistant and Susceptible Strain of Mosquito Fish. *Trans. Amer. Fish. Soc.* 95: 335-344.

Fukuto T.R. 1971. Relationship between the Structure of OP Compound and their Activity as Acetocholinesterase Inhibitors. *Bull. W.H.O.* 44: 31-42.

Holden A.V. 1962. The Absorption of C14 Labeled DDT from Water by Fish. *Ann. Appl. Biol.* 50: 467-477.

Janardhan Rao M. 1991. Effect of Salinity and the Pesticide Endosulfan on the Physiology of M. Sallei, Ph.D. Thesis.Andhra University, Waltair.

Khillare Y.K. and Wagh S.B. 1987. Effect of Malathion on Level of Ascorbic Acid in Fresh Water Fish, *Barbusticto* (Ham). *J. Adv. Zool.* 7 (2): 105-107.

Kushwaha B., Srivastava S.K. Singh B., Nagpure N.S., Ponniah A.G. 2000. Evaluation of Comet Assay and Micronucleus Test as Genotoxic Assay in *Channapunctatus. Natl. Acad. Sci. Lett.* 23 (11/12): 177-179.

Lomte, V.S., Jadhav, M.J. 1982. Studies on Respiratory Metabolism in the Freshwater Bivalve *Lamellidenescorrianus, Life. Sci. Adv.* 1(1): 5-8.

Maheshwari U.K., Maheswari N., Sharma A., Das R.C., Hussain Z. Sharma P.P., Singh A.J. and Raj B. 2001. Toxicity of an Organophosphate Pesticide Triarophios on an Air Breathing Fish *Clariusbatrachus*(Linn) and Species Related MATC in the Aquatic Environment. *J. Envi. Res.* 11(2): 97-100.

Malla Reddy P. 1988. Effect of Fenvalerate and Cypermethrin on the Oxygen Consumption of Fish, *Cypriruscarpio J. Mendel.* 20: 209-211.

Murphy S.D. 1980. Toxicology In: The basic Science of Poisons, 2nd Edn. Macmillan. Publishing Company, Inc. New York.

Nagrathnamma R. and Ramanmurthi R. 1982. Metabolic Depression in the Fresh Water Teleost, *cyprinuscarpio* Exposed to an Organophosphate Pesticide *Current. Sci.* 51(13): 668-669.

Nataranjan G.M. 1981. Changes in the Bimodal Gas Exchange and some Blood Parameters in the Air Breathing Fish, *Channastraitus* (Bleeker) following Lethal (LC_{50}/48hours) Exposure to Metasystox (Demeton). *Curr. Sci.* 50: 40-41.

O'Brien, R.D. 1967. Insecticides Action and Metabolism, Academic Press New York and London.

Qaisur Rahman and Sadhu D.N. 2009. Effect of Pesticides on Aquatic and Aerial on Oxygen Consumption in an Air Breathing Murrelfish *Channagachua.Nat. Env. Poll. Tech.* 8(3): 603-608

Qaisur Rahman 2011. Studies on some Factors Affecting Aerial and Aquatic Respiration in an Air Breathing Fish *Channagachua.* Ph.D. Thesis, Vinoba Bhave University, Hazaribagh, Jharkhand, India.

Rao J.V., Ranic H.S., Kavita, P., Rao, R.N. and Madhavendra S.S. 2003. Toxicity of Chlorophyrifos to the Fish, *Oreochromismossambicus Bull. Environ. Contom.Toxicol.* 70: 985-992.

Saroja K. 1959. Oxygen Consumption in Relation to Body Size and Temperature in the Earthworm, *Megascolexmarutii* when kept Submerged under Water. *Proc. Indian. Acad. of Sci.* 49: 183-193.

T. Anita Susan, Sobha., K. and Tilak K.S. 2010. A Study on Acute Toxicity, Oxygen Consumption and Behavioural Changes in the Three Major Carps, *Labeorohita (ham), Catla Catla*(Ham) *and cirrhinusmrigala* (Ham) Exposed to Fenvalerate, *Bioresearch. Bulletin.* 1: 33-40.

Verma S.R. and Dalela R.C. 1975. Studies on Pollution of Kalinadi by Industrial Wastes near Mansurpur. Part II Biological Index of Pollution and Biological Chanacterstic of the River. *Acta. Hydrobiol.* 3(25): 259-274.

Vineetkumar K. Patil and David M. 2008. Behaviour and Respiratory Dysfunction as an Index of Malathion Toxicity in the Fresh Water Fish, *Labeorohita* (Hamilton). *Turkish J. Fisheries.Aquatic. Sci.* 8: 233-237.

Vutukuru S.S. 2005. Acute Effects of Hexavalent Chromium on Survial, Oxygen Consumption Hematological Parameters and some Biochemical Profiles of Indian Major Carp, *Labeorohita. Int. J. Envi. Res. Publ. Health.* 2: 456-462

Welsh J.H, and Smith R.I. (1960). Laboratory Exercise in Invertebrate Physiology.

Welch, P.S.1948. Limnological methods. Mc. Graw Hill Co. Inc. New York, London. 20-213 pp.

Wilkinson C.F. and Denison M.S. 1982. Pesticides Interactions with Biotransformation Systems In: Effects of Chronic Exposure to Pesticides on Animal System (Ed.) Chambers, J.E. and Yarbrough, J.D.) Raven Press, New York. 1-24 pp.

Pages: 134-142

Renewable Resources and Environment

Edited by: Dr. Baby Tabassum

ISBN: 978-93-5056-893-4

Edition: 2018

Published by: Discovery Publishing House Pvt. Ltd., New Delhi (India)

Solid Waste Management

Challenging Environmental Issue in India

Suman Lata

ABSTRACT

In India due to over population, industrialization, urbanization and economic growth especially in the last few decades has also resulted in a rapid increase in both domestic and industrial waste, the main driver for domestic waste is the rapid urbanisation that is slated to change India from a largely rural to a majority urban country in the next decade. In present our country has been faces a big problem of solid waste management. So in this paper we give some methods used for MSW, some rules of Indian government to resolve the problem of MSW, etc.

INTRODUCTION

Solid-waste management, is the technique of the collecting, treating, and disposing of solid material that is discarded because it has served its purpose or is no longer in use. Improper disposal of municipal solid waste can create unsanitary conditions, and these conditions in turn can lead to environmental pollution. The tasks of solid-waste management present complex technical challenges. They also pose a wide variety of administrative, economic, and social problems that must be managed and solved.

Assistant Professor, Department of Physics, Govt. Raza P.G. College, Rampur (U.P.) (India)

Solid waste can broadly be classified into two categories. According to Indian MSW, Rules 2000 "Municipal Solid Waste" includes commercial and domestic wastes generated in a municipal or notified area in either solid or semi-solid form excluding industrial hazardous wastes but including treated bio-medical wastes. Solid waste also includes hazardous waste generated by various industries. Municipal Solid Waste (MSW) can further be classified into biodegradable waste (such as food and kitchen waste); recyclable materials (such as paper, glass, bottles, metals and certain plastics) and domestic hazardous waste (such as medication, chemicals, light bulbs and batteries).

METHODS

Some methods used in solid waste management are:

1. **Sanitary Land Filling:** In a sanitary landfill, garbage is spread out in thin layers, compacted and covered with clay or plastic foam. In the modern landfills the bottom is covered with an impermeable liner, usually several layers of clay, thick plastic and sand. The liner protects the ground water from being contaminated due to percolation of leachate. Leachate from bottom is pumped and sent for treatment. When landfill is full it is covered with clay, sand, gravel and top soil to prevent seepage of water. Several wells are drilled near the landfill site to monitor if any leakage is contaminating ground water. Methane produced by anaerobic decomposition is collected and burnt to produce electricity or heat.
2. **Incineration:** Incineration is a disposal method in which solid organic wastes are subjected to combustion so as to convert them into residue and gaseous products. This method is useful for disposal of residue of both solid waste management and solid residue from waste water management. This process reduces the volumes of solid waste to 20 to 30 per cent of the original volume. Incineration and other high temperature waste treatment systems are sometimes described as "thermal treatment".

Incinerators convert waste materials into heat, gas, steam and ash. Incineration is carried out both on a small scale by individuals and on a large scale by industry. It is used to dispose of solid, liquid and gaseous waste. It is recognized as a practical method of disposing of certain hazardous waste materials. Incineration is a controversial method of waste disposal, due to issues such as emission of gaseous pollutants.

3. **Compositing:** Composting is a biological process in which micro-organisms, mainly fungi and bacteria, convert degradable organic waste into humus like substance. This finished product, which looks like soil, is high in carbon and nitrogen and is an excellent medium for growing plants.The process of composting ensures the waste that is produced in the kitchens is not carelessly thrown and left to rot. It recycles the nutrients and returns them to the soil as nutrients. Apart from being clean, cheap, and safe, composting can significantly reduce the amount of disposable garbage.
4. **Pyrolysis:** Pyrolysis is a form of incineration that chemically decomposes organic materials by heat in the absence of oxygen. Pyrolysis typically occurs under pressure and at operating temperatures above 430 °C (800 °F).

RULES FOR SOLID WASTE MANAGEMENT

Minister of State (Independent Charge) of Environment, Forest and Climate Change, Shri Prakash Javadekar in 05 April 2016 said that Solid Waste Management Rules Revised After 16 Years; Rules Now Extend to Urban and Industrial Areas.

(I) Salient features of SWM Rules, 2016 include:

1. The Rules are now applicable beyond Municipal areas and extend to urban agglomerations, census towns, notified industrial townships, areas under the control of Indian Railways, airports, airbase, Port and harbour, defence establishments, special economic zones, State and Central government organizations, places of pilgrims, religious & historical importance.

2. The source segregation of waste has been mandated to channelize the waste to wealth by recovery, reuse and recycle.
3. Responsibilities of Generators have been introduced to segregate waste in to three streams, Wet (Biodegradable), Dry (Plastic, Paper, metal, wood, etc.) and domestic hazardous wastes (diapers, napkins, empty containers of cleaning agents, mosquito repellents, etc.) and handover segregated wastes to authorized rag-pickers or waste collectors or local bodies.
4. Integration of waste pickers/ragpickers and waste dealers/Kabadiwalas in the formal system should be done by State Governments, and Self Help Group, or any other group to be formed.
5. No person should throw, burn, or bury the solid waste generated by him, on streets, open public spaces outside his premises, or in the drain, or water bodies.
6. Generator will have to pay 'User Fee' to waste collector and for 'Spot Fine' for Littering and Non-segregation.
7. Used sanitary waste like diapers, sanitary pads should be wrapped securely in pouches provided by manufacturers or brand owners of these products or in a suitable wrapping material and shall place the same in the bin meant for dry waste/non-bio-degradable waste.
8. The concept of partnership in Swachh Bharat has been introduced. Bulk and institutional generators, market associations, event organizers and hotels and restaurants have been made directly responsible for segregation and sorting the waste and manage in partnership with local bodies.
9. All hotels and restaurants should segregate bio-degradable waste and set up a system of collection or follow the system of collection set up by local body to ensure that such food waste is utilized for composting/biomethanation.

10. All Resident Welfare and market Associations, Gated communities and institution with an area >5,000 sq. m should segregate waste at source- in to valuable dry waste like plastic, tin, glass, paper, etc. and handover recyclable material to either the authorized waste pickers or the authorized recyclers, or to the urban local body.
11. The bio-degradable waste should be processed, treated and disposed of through composting or bio-methanation within the premises as far as possible. The residual waste shall be given to the waste collectors or agency as directed by the local authority.
12. New townships and Group Housing Societies have been made responsible to develop in-house waste handling, and processing arrangements for bio-degradable waste.
13. Every street vendor should keep suitable containers for storage of waste generated during the course of his activity such as food waste, disposable plates, cups, cans, wrappers, coconut shells, leftover food, vegetables, fruits etc. and deposit such waste at waste storage depot or container or vehicle as notified by the local authority.
14. The developers of Special Economic Zone, industrial estate, industrial park to earmark at least 5% of the total area of the plot or minimum 5 plots/sheds for recovery and recycling facility.
15. All manufacturers of disposable products such as tin, glass, plastics packaging etc. or brand owners who introduce such products in the market shall provide necessary financial assistance to local authorities for the establishment of waste management system.
16. All such brand owners who sale or market their products in such packaging material which are non-biodegradable should put in place a system to collect back the packaging waste generated due to their production.
17. Manufacturers or Brand Owners or marketing companies of sanitary napkins and diapers should explore the possibility of using all recyclable materials in their

products or they shall provide a pouch or wrapper for disposal of each napkin or diapers along with the packet of their sanitary products.

18. All such manufacturers, brand owners or marketing companies should educate the masses for wrapping and disposal of their products.
19. All industrial units using fuel and located within 100 km from a solid waste based RDF plant shall make arrangements within six months from the date of notification of these rules to replace at least 5% of their fuel requirement by RDF so produced.
20. Non-recyclable waste having calorific value of 1500 K/cal/kg or more shall not be disposed of on landfills and shall only be utilized for generating energy either or through refuse derived fuel or by giving away as feed stock for preparing refuse derived fuel.
21. High calorific wastes shall be used for co-processing in cement or thermal power plants.
22. Construction and demolition waste should be stored, separately disposed off, as per the Construction and Demolition Waste Management Rules, 2016.
23. Horticulture waste and garden waste generated from his premises should be disposed as per the directions of local authority.
24. An event, or gathering organiser of more than 100 persons at any licensed/ unlicensed place, should ensure segregation of waste at source and handing over of segregated waste to waste collector or agency, as specified by local authority.
25. Special provision for management of solid waste in hilly areas:- Construction of landfill on the hill shall be avoided. A transfer station at a suitable enclosed location shall be setup to collect residual waste from the processing facility and inert waste. Suitable land shall be identified in the plain areas, down the hill, within 25

kilometers for setting up sanitary landfill. The residual waste from the transfer station shall be disposed off at this sanitary landfill.

26. In case of non-availability of such land, efforts shall be made to set up regional sanitary landfill for the inert and residual waste.

(II) Municipal Solid Waste

With the ever increasing population and urbanization, the waste management has emerged as a huge challenge in the country. Not only the waste has increased in quantity, but the characteristics of waste have also changed tremendously over a period, with the introduction of so many new gadgets and equipment. It is estimated that about 62 million tonnes of waste is generated annually in the country, out of which 5.6 million is plastic waste, 0.17 million is biomedical waste. In addition, hazardous waste generation is 7.90 million TPA and 15 lakh tonne is e-waste. The per capita waste generation in Indian cities range from 200 grams to 600 grams per day (2011). 43 million TPA is collected, 11.9 million is treated and 31 million is dumped in landfill sites.

(III) Proper Solid Waste Management

Scientific disposal of solid waste through segregation, collection and treatment and disposal in an environmentally sound manner minimises the adverse impact on the environment. The local authorities are responsible for the development of infrastructure for collection, storage, segregation, transportation, processing and disposal of MSW.

As per information available for 2013-14, compiled by CPCB, municipal authorities have so far only set up 553 compost & vermi-compost plants, 56 bio-methanation plants, 22 RDF plants and 13 Waste to Energy (W to E) plants in the country.

(IV) Problems of Unscientific MSW Disposal

Only about 75-80% of the municipal waste gets collected and out of this only 22-28% is processed and treated and remaining is disposed of indiscriminately at dump yards. It is projected that by the year 2031 the MSW generation shall increase to 165 million tonnes and to 436 million tons by 2050. If cities continue to dump the waste at present rate without treatment, it will need 1240 hectares of land per year and with projected generation of 165 million tons of waste by 2031, the requirement of setting up of land fil for 20 years of 10 meters height will require 66,000 hectares of land.

As per the Report of the Task Force of erstwhile Planning Commission, the untapped waste has a potential of generating 439 MW of power from 32,890 TPD of combustible wastes including Refused Derived Fuel (RDF), 1.3 million cubic metre of biogas per day, or 72 MW of electricity from biogas and 5.4 million metric tonnes of compost annually to support agriculture.

(V) Consultation process for new Solid Waste Rules

The draft Solid Waste Management Rules were published in June, 2015 inviting public objections and suggestions. Stakeholders consultation meets were organized in New Delhi, Mumbai and Kolkata. Consultative meetings with relevant Central Ministries, State Governments, State Pollution Control Boards and major hospitals were also held. The suggestions/objections (about 111) received were examined by the Working Group in the Ministry. Based on the recommendations of the Working Group, the Ministry has published the Solid Waste Management Rules, 2016.

SUGGESTIONS FOR SUCCESSFUL MSW MANAGEMENT

Do	Do Not
Undertake an integrated strategic planning process	Rush into investments in new equipment without putting them into a strategic context
Ensure wide support for the planning process and the results	Confine consultation to an elite group
Ensure that the target service level is affordable	Base choices on what is supposedly the most "advanced" technology, but is affordable only by a minority

(Contd...)

Undertake a detailed study of the existing situation	Duplicate existing studies
Measure key factors in your city as a basis for decisions	Rely on the literature for big decisions
Apply an impartial process to select options on the basis of benefits	Sign up with a specific commercial vendor without considering all the options
Do detailed analysis of costs	Underestimate costs or overestimate revenues
Separate responsibility for providing the service from day-to-day service deliverable	Delegate responsibility for a key public service to the private sector, though they may do day-to-day delivery
Consider private sector delivery as an option	Forget the conditions for success: competition, transparency and accountability
Consider different options for user charges to cover the shortfall in revenues	Apply user charges without considering the needs of the poor for solid waste management services
Improve performance of collection, sweeping and transport services	Buy costly "high-tech" vehicles
Introduce preventative maintenance for vehicles	Tolerate a high percentage of vehicles in for service at any one time
Give priority to extending services to unserviced areas	Forget about health risks to the whole population of uncollected solid waste

REFERENCES

"Guidance on Solid Waste Magement" https://www.gdrc.org/uem/waste/waste management.html, Source - Cities Solution Network 2001.

"Municipal Solid Waste Management in Indian Cities – A Review"; Waste Management 2008, Vol. 28, pp. 459-467.

Press Report, Government of India, Ministry of Environment and Forest (MoEF), 05 April 2016.

"Scenario of Solid Waste Management in Present Indian Context"; R. Rajput *et.al*; Caspian J. Env. Sci. 2009, Vol. 7, pp. 45-53.

"Waste rules in India", Article by Chintan, Environmental Research and Action Group (www.chintan-india.org)

Pages: **143-163**

Renewable Resources and Environment
Edited by: **Dr. Baby Tabassum**
ISBN: 978-93-5056-893-4
Edition: **2018**
Published by: **Discovery Publishing House Pvt. Ltd., New Delhi (India)**

Recent Advances in Developments of Synthetic Anti-Cancer Agents for Treatment and Prevention of Breast and Endometrial Cancer

Shahla Nusrat Kidwai[†]; Sahadev[†]
Mohd Kamil Hussain[†*]

ABSTRACT

Perhaps no malady affecting women in the modern world instills more panic than breast cancer, which strikes fear into the female's heart, generating a deep sense of powerlessness. Recent statistics shows that breast cancer is the most commonly diagnosed cancer among women in all the regions of the world, accounting for 29% of all new cancers and 15% of all cancer deaths in women. Several targeted therapies, and anti-estrogen therapies, have greatly improved patient outcomes. A much more detailed understanding of the underlying biology that drives malignant progression and metastases has yielded other novel targets including PI3K/ Mtor, PARP, HSP90, HDAC and human DNA ligase I (hligI) which are currently being tested. With the emergence of drug resistance as a major new impediment in cancer treatment, combined with the problems of low tumour selectivity, diversity of types of cancer and drug toxicity, there is an urgent need for the discovery of less toxic and more potent,

† Department of Chemistry, Govt. Raza Post Graduate, Collage, Rampur - 244 901 (U.P.) (India)

* *Corresponding author:* Mohd Kamil Hussain Email: mkhcdri@gmail.com

new anti- cancer drugs, which selectively target the interactive mechanisms involved in growth and metastasis of cancer without harming the healthy body cells.

INTRODUCTION

Cancer is a word that strikes fear into people's hearts, producing a deep sense of helplessness. It is a major public health problem worldwide, having a profound impact on society. The most common cancers in 2016 are projected to be breast cancer, lung and bronchus cancer, prostate cancer, colon and rectum cancer, bladder cancer, melanoma of the skin, non-Hodgkin lymphoma, thyroid cancer, kidney and renal pelvis cancer, leukaemia, endometrial cancer, and pancreatic cancer. Breast cancer is the most commonly diagnosed cancer and the second leading cause of cancer death among women.[1] An estimated 1.7 million women will be diagnosed with breast cancer in 2020, which is 26% increase from current levels.[2]

Breast cancer is a heterogeneous disease and is classified on the basis of presence or absence of estrogen receptors (ERs). ER+ breast cancer accounts for 80% and ER - negative breast cancer accounts for 20-30% of total breast cancer cases. Most breast cancers are invasive, or infiltrating.[3-4]

India is experiencing an unprecedented rise in the number of breast cancer cases across all sections of society; it is the most common cancer in most cities in India. Breast cancer accounts for 25% to 32% of all female cancers in top most cities such as Mumbai, Delhi, Bengaluru, Bhopal, Kolkata, Chennai, Ahmedabad. India has one of the worst survivals from breast cancer, in the world and has the highest number of women dying from breast cancer in the world as Indian society is so deep rooted in myths and alternative treatment and unusual illogical beliefs.[5a]

CANCER DRUGS APPROVED BY THE FOOD AND DRUG ADMINISTRATION (FDA) FOR BREAST CANCER

Evista (Raloxifene Hydrochloride), Nolvadex (Tamoxifen Citrate), Abitrexate (Methotrexate), Ado-Trastuzumab Emtansine, Afinitor (Everolimus), Anastrozole, Aredia

(Pamidronate Disodium), Arimidex (Anastrozole), Aromasin (Exemestane), Capecitabine, Clafen (Cyclophosphamide), Cyclophosphamide, Docetaxel, Doxorubicin Hydrochloride, Ellence (Epirubicin Hydrochloride), Epirubicin Hydrochloride, Eribulin Mesylate, Everolimus, Exemestane, 5-FU (Fluorouracil Injection), Fareston (Toremifene), Faslodex (Fulvestrant), Femara (Letrozole), Fulvestrant, Gemcitabine Hydrochloride, Gemzar (Gemcitabine Hydrochloride), Goserelin Acetate, Ibrance (Palbociclib), Ixabepilone, Lapatinib Ditosylate, Letrozole, Megestrol Acetate, Paclitaxel, Paclitaxel Albumin-stabilized Nanoparticle Formulation, Palbociclib, Pamidronate Disodium, Pertuzumab, Thiotepa, Toremifene, Tykerb (Lapatinib Ditosylate), Velban (Vinblastine Sulfate), Xeloda (Capecitabine), Zoladex (Goserelin Acetate).**Source:* Natinal Cancer Institute USA[5b]

BIOLOGICAL THERAPIES FOR BREAST CANCER

Estrogen Receptor Modulators

"Estrogens" are a family of related molecules that controls many aspects of human physiology, including development, reproduction and homeostasis. The natural estrogens are steroid molecules, which mean that they are derived from a particular type of molecular skeleton containing four rings of carbon atoms, giving the shape shown in (Fig. 15.1).

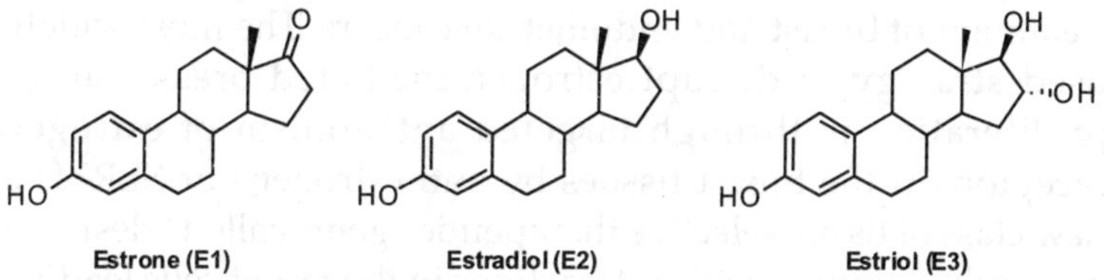

Estrone (E1) Estradiol (E2) Estriol (E3)

Fig. 15.1: Structure of Estrogen molecules

The most prevalent forms of human estrogen are estrone (E1), estradiol (E2) and estriol (E3). Estriol is the weakest form of estrogen and produced by the placenta during pregnancy. It does not appear to affect the bones, breast, brain, heart, and other organs the way estradiol does, and is therefore not likely to ameliorate cognitive and mood disorders. In premenopausal women, (E1) and (E2) are secreted primarily by the ovaries during the menstrual cycle, with minor levels derived from adipose tissue and the adrenal glands. Estrone is produced in fat cells postmenopausal women. 17β-Estradiol (E2) stimulates the development and maintenance of female characteristics and sexual reproduction with multiple physiological processes in women.[6-9]

The steroid hormone estrogen mediates a number of biological processes that range from reproductive health to bone maintenance through estrogen receptor (ER) a member of a large superfamily of nuclear receptors (NR).[10] The same estrogen is also predominantly involved in the initiation and proliferation of ER+ve breast cancer and much efforts are now being devoted to block estrogen formation and action. The ER exists in two isoforms, α (ERα) and β (ERβ), both of which are ligand induced transcription factors that have different distributions in various estrogen target tissues and also have different functions, some of which have not yet been clarified. ERα the predominant subtype expressed in breast cancer induces proliferation in response to estrogen, while ERβ the predominant subtype present in bone, colon, prostrate inhibits proliferation of breast cancer cells by antagonizing the function of ERα and also checks osteoporosis, thus ERα and ERβ are potential target for treatment of breast and endometrial cancers. The most widely used strategy to disrupt estrogen mediated breast cancer proliferation is through targeted antagonism of estrogen receptors in the breast tissues by anti estrogens or SERMs a new class of tissue selective therapeutic agents called "designer molecules" with specific interactions in the target cells leading to tissue selective actions.

Many ER-ligands have shown mixed agonist-antagonist and tissue-selective activities that are useful in post-menopausal hormone replacement therapy, in fertility regulation and most importantly in the prevention and treatment of breast cancer. The estrogen ligand pharmacophore model (fig. 15.2) clearly defines binding affinity of ligand with estrogen receptors and their character as agonist and antagonists[4, 11-13]

On the basis of ligand pharmacophore model, libraries of ER-subtype selective ligands Hussain *et al.* have synthesized a library of several new coumarin and chromene prototype derivatives (fig. 15.2) and evaluated for their ERα and ERβ selective activity. Coumarin prototype compounds were found to be ERα selective and the most active exhibiting potential antiproliferative activity against both ER+ve & ER-ve breast cancer cell lines (1 and 2). The surprise finding of the series however, was the novel prototype III chromenes with aroyl substitution at the 6th position (3).

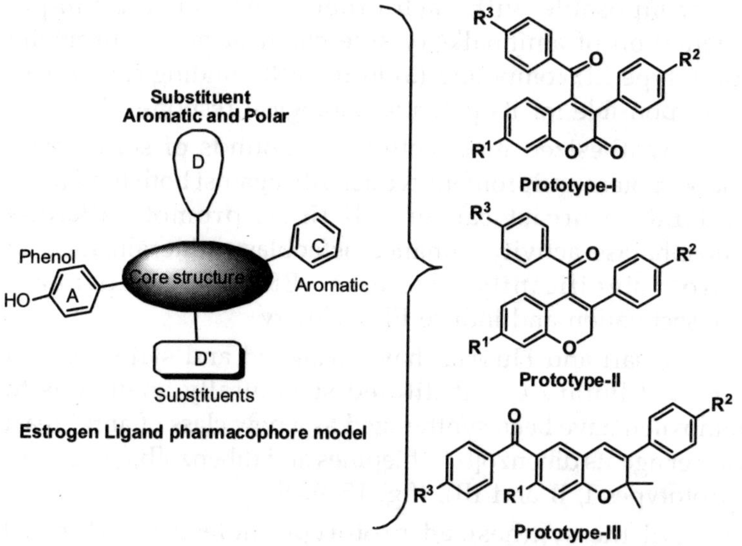

Fig. 15.2: Designing of ERα and ERβ selective ligands (Hussain *et al.* 2014)

Both the compounds have shown potent antiproliferative activity against both the breast cancer cell lines, promote alkaline phosphatase activity, enhance osteoblast minerali-zation in vitro, significantly decrease ERE-ERα dependant transactivation and induce ERβ activity. This specific upregulation of ERβ isoform activity of compound 1 may be responsible for the antiosteoporotic activity at picomolar concentration. In addition, both the compounds were also devoid of any estrogenic activity which correlates to their antiestrogenic behaviour in the two breast cancer cell lines (MCF-7 and MDA-MB 231).

Assessment of selectivity using specific SiRNAs for ERα and ERβ revealed that most of the compounds showed ERα and ERβ- mediated action. Computational docking analyses of most active compounds was conducted to correlate the interaction with the two receptors and it was found that the docked conformations of the coumarin prototype, compound (1) at ERα and ERβ active sites were more or less superimposable with each other. However, the unique orientation of aminoalkoxy side chain of novel chromene (prototype III) compound (3) in the ERβ binding cavity may be responsible for its potential biological response.[4]

Synthesized most active compounds of series have shown potent antiproliferative activity against both the ER+ve and ER-ve breast cancer cell lines, promote alkaline phosphatase activity, enhance osteoblast mineralization in vitro, significantly decrease ERE-ERα dependant transactivation and induce ERβ activity.

Ansari and Hussain have designed and synthesized a targeted library of substituted structurally analogous to tamoxifen have been synthesized as a new class of anti-breast cancer agents dibenzo[b,f] thiepines and dibenzo[b,f] oxepines (prototypes I, II and III), (fig. 15.3).[14]

All the synthesized prototype molecules exhibited potential antiproliferative activity against both the ER+ve and ER-ve breast cancer cell lines. Of all the compound tested, 6 exhibited potent in-vitro antiproliferative activity at 1.33 μM and 5 μM concentration in MCF-7 and MDA-MB-231 cell lines and was devoid of any cytotoxicity in normal HEK cells even at 50 μM. Cell cycle analysis showed that the compound 6 inhibited cell proliferation due to G0/G1 arrest in MCF-7 cells.

Annexin-V FITC and PI staining experiments confirmed that the cell inhibition was primarily due to apoptosis and not by necrosis, which was also supported by LDH release assay experiment.

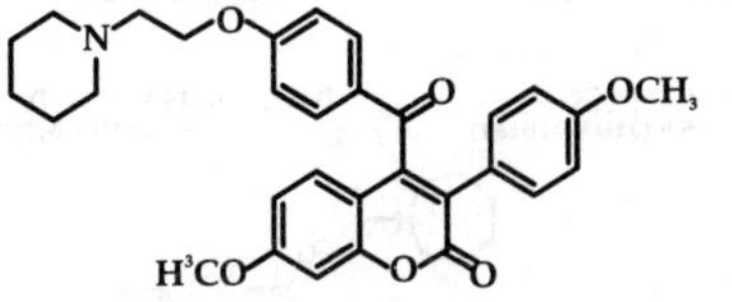

1
IC_{50} values (μM): 5.7 (MCF-7) 12.7 (MDA-MB 231), 0.16% RBA

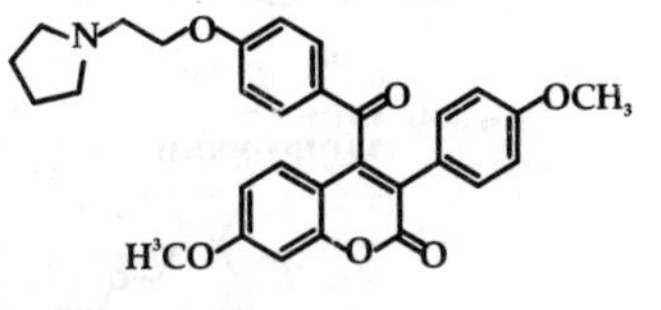

2
IC_{50} values (μM): 16.3 (MCF-7) 18.8 (MDA-MB 231), 1.3% RBA

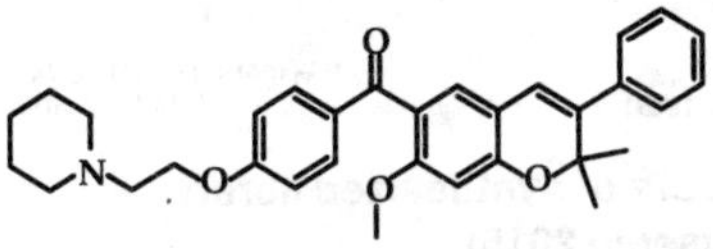

3
IC_{50} values (μM): 6.8 (MCF-7) 16.9 (MDA-MB 231), 17.7 Ishikawa, 0.225% RBA

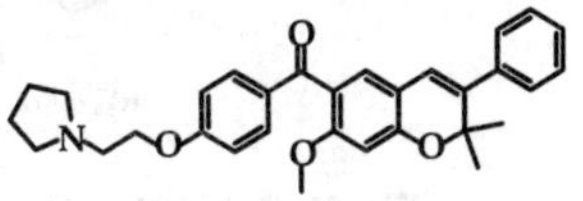

4
IC_{50} values (μM): 8.1 (MCF-7) 14.8 (MDA-MB 231), 16.9 Ishikawa, 0.6% RBA

Fig. 15.3: Most active members of synthesized library (Hussain *et al.* 2014)

Molecular docking studies showed better binding interaction of the new dibenzo[b,f] thiepine analogue 6 with the estrogen receptor (ER) as compared to 4-hydroxy-tamoxifen and this enhanced binding might be responsible for its estrogen antagonistic activity that induces cell cycle arrest, apoptosis and inhibition of breast cancer cells. Other compounds 5, 7, 8 and 9 efficiently inhibited the proliferation of breast cancer cells (fig. 15.5).

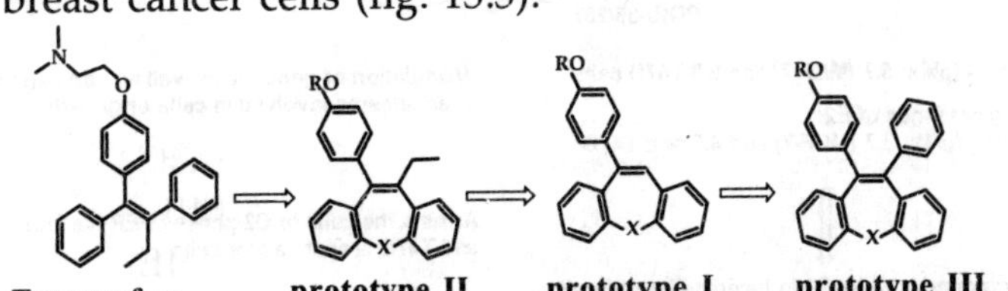

Tamoxefen | **prototype II X = O and S** | **prototype I X = O and S** | **prototype III X = O and S**

Fig. 15.4: Deigning of dibenzo[b,f] thiepines and dibenzo[b,f] oxepines (Ansari & Hussain 2015)

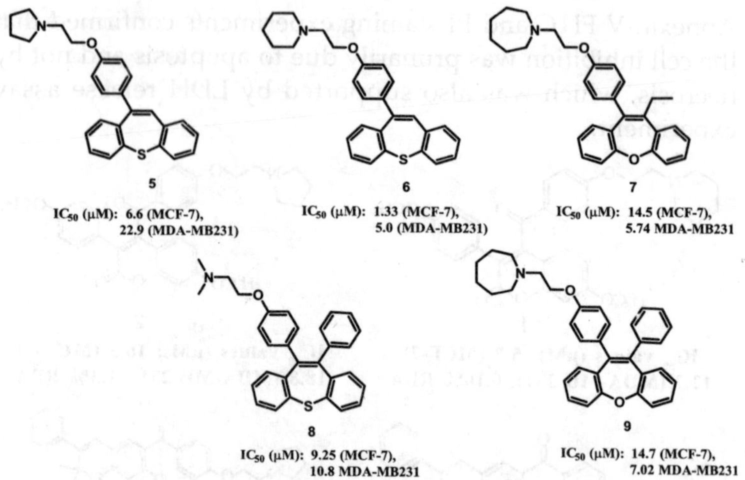

5
IC_{50} (μM): 6.6 (MCF-7), 22.9 (MDA-MB231)

6
IC_{50} (μM): 1.33 (MCF-7), 5.0 (MDA-MB231)

7
IC_{50} (μM): 14.5 (MCF-7), 5.74 MDA-MB231

8
IC_{50} (μM): 9.25 (MCF-7), 10.8 MDA-MB231

9
IC_{50} (μM): 14.7 (MCF-7), 7.02 MDA-MB231

Fig 15.5: Most active members of synthesized library (Ansari & Hussain 2015)

2,3-Diaryl-2H-1-benzopyrans serve as anti-breast cancer and anti endometrial cancer activities. 2,3-diaryl benzopyran compounds have been synthesized and identified as potent anti-estrogen at uterine level. CDRI-85/287 (2-[piperidino-ethoxyphenyl]-3-phenyl-2H-benzo(b)pyran) (1C) exhibits significant anti-breast cancer activity via modulation of genomic as well as non-genomic mechanisms involved in cellular growth and arrested the cells in G2 phase in ER+ve MCF-7 and T47D breast cancer cells.

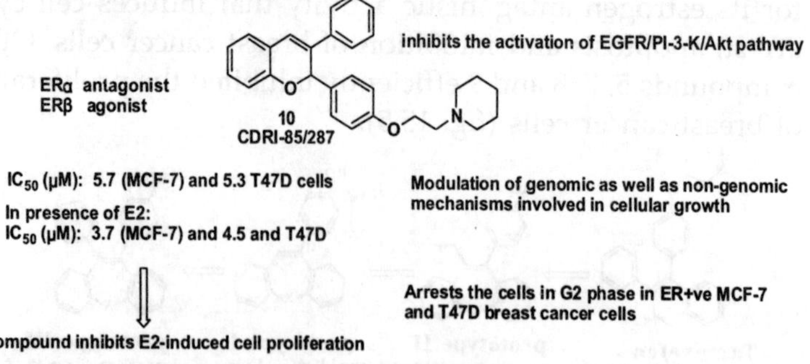

Fig. 15.6: CDRI-85/287 (2-[piperidinoethoxyphenyl]-3-phenyl-2H-benzo(b)pyran) (Saxena & Hussain 2013)

The significant in vivo efficacy in animal model suggests that CDRI-85/287 can serve as therapeutic agent for treatment of estrogen-dependent breast cancer. Transactivation studies in ERα/ERβ -transfected MDA-MB231 cells suggested that at cyclin D1 promoter, compound antagonized the action of ERα-mediated estradiol (E_2) response while acted as estrogen agonist via ERβ. The expression of cell cycle inhibitory protein p21 was increased leading to G2/M phase arrest. In parallel, compound also interfered with EGFR activation, caused inhibition of PI-3-K/Akt pathway and subsequent induction of apoptosis via intrinsic pathway. This study concluded that benzopyran derivative CDRI-85/287 induces G2-M arrest in estrogen receptor-positive breast cancer cells via modulation of estrogen receptors α (ERα) and β (ERβ) -mediated signaling, in parallel to EGFR signaling and suppresses the growth of tumor xenograft.[15]

Phenolic analogue (K-1) of CDRI-85/287, display potent antiestrogenic and apoptosis-inducing activity in rat uterine hyperplasia. K-1 inhibits endometrial proliferation via nonclassical estrogen receptor signaling mechanisms. It interfered with Akt activation and induced apoptosis via the intrinsic pathway and inhibited estradiol-induced hyperplasia formation in rat uterus. Result suggests that benzopyran 11 compound is a potent apoptosis inducer in the uterus uterus and can be used as therapeutic agent for endometrial hyperplasia.[16]

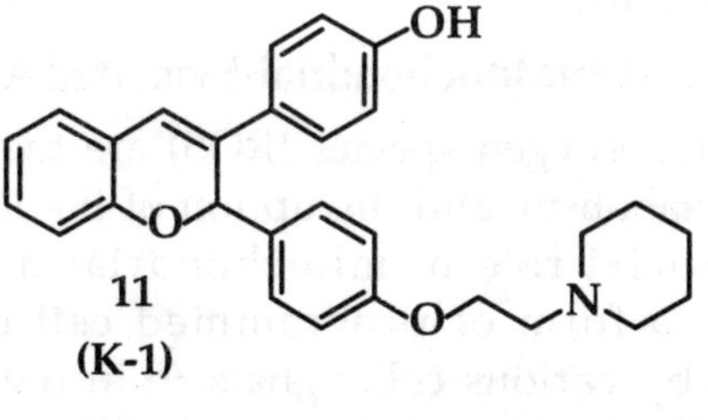

OH

O

11

(K-1)

O

N

Fig. 15.7: 2-[piperidinoethoxyphenyl]-3-[4-hydroxyphenyl]-2H-benzo(b)pyran (K-1). (Chandra, Saxena, Fatima and Hussin *et al.* 2011, 2013, 2014)

2-[piperidinoethoxyphenyl]-3-[4-hydroxyphenyl]-2H-benzo(b)pyran (K-1) inhibits the binding of estradiol (E2) to human ERα and ERβ competitively and inhibit proliferative activity of human endometrial Ishikawa, HEC1B and primary endometrial adenocarcinoma cell lines. It induced ER-mediated transactivation of the cyclin-dependent kinase inhibitor (CDKI) p21WAF-1in both COS-1 cells and in Ishikawa cells. Results indicate that the compound K-1 suppressed the cellular growth via ERβ agonism, induction of p21 and via promoting the ERα-β heterodimerization, Results demonstrats that the dual action of 11 (K-1) may be of significant therapeutic value in ERα and ERβ +ve cases of endometrial cancer.[17]

Chandra and Hussain have reported that compound 11 (K-1) induce apoptosis by increasing the expression of apoptotic markers and reducing the expression of p-CREB and BclxL. Compound interfered with GPR30-regulated-EGFR activation, decreased p-ERK, p-c-jun, c-fos, cyclinD1 and c-myc expression. K-1 significantly decrease the volume and weight of tumor *in* tumor-bearing mice.[18]

Chandra and Hussain, reported that compound 11 (K-1) significantly down regulates the Wnt/β-catenin signaling which might be considered as one of the mechanisms responsible for specific anti-proliferative activity of K-1 in human endometrial hyperplasial cells. Experimental data demonstrate that K-1 can serve as a future therapeutic agent for treatment of endometrial hyperplasia over the currently available therapy.[19]

ROS-IndependentMitochondrial-Mediated Apoptosis

Reactive oxygen species (ROS) are the by-products of cellular metabolism, and disruption of the ROS homeostasis plays a crucial role in mitochondrial dysfunction and apoptosis, a form of programmed cell death which is controlled by various cell signals.[20] In the mitochondrial-mediated intrinsic pathway of apoptosis, disruption of mitochondrial membrane results in the release of cytochrome c and the subsequent activation of caspase-9, leading to cleavage of the executioner caspase-3 and/or -7.[21] ROS can also activate the mitochondrial membrane permeability and induce loss of mitochondrial transmembrane potential. Various findings suggest that increased ROS-driven apoptosis pathway kill cancer cells, whereas many studies support that decreased ROS level induces apoptosis.[21-24]

Ansari and Hussain synthesized and evaluated a library of 3, 4, 6-triaryl-2-pyridones for their anti-breast cancer activity, in vitro in ER+ve and ER-ve cancer cell lines, wherein, compounds 12 (4-(3, 4-dimethoxyphenyl)-6-(4-methoxyphenyl)-3-phenylpyridin-2(1H)-one) and 13 (3,6-bis (4-methoxyphenyl)-4-(4-(2-(piperidin-1-yl) ethoxy) phenyl) pyridin-2(1H)-one) were found to be the most active with best safety profile towards non-cancer originated HEK-293 cell lines. Compounds 12 and 13 induced statistically significant arrest of cells in G1 phase and reduction in S-phase cells in a dose-dependent manner. Compound 12, unlike compound 13 exerts breast cancer cell membrane specific action, whereas compound 13 induced ROS-independent mitochondrial-mediated apoptosis in MDA-MB-231 breast cancer cell line. Compound 13 was found about five times safer than its effective IC_{50} values in MDA-MB-231 cell line, which makes it a non-toxic breast cancer therapeutic agent.[25]

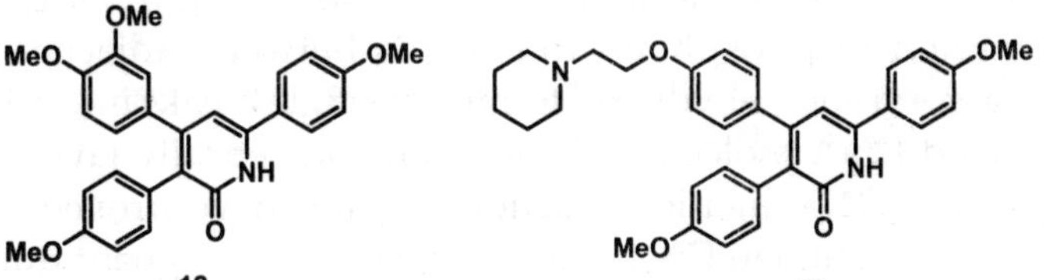

OMe MeO OMe NH O MeO 12

N O OMe NH O MeO 13

Fig.15.8: 3, 4, 6-triaryl-2-Pyridone: A Non toxic anti-cancer agents (Ansari & Hussain 2016)

Human DNA Ligase I Inhibitors

Living organisms maintain their genomic integrity through DNA replication. DNA ligases play a vital and indispensible role in all DNA replication and repair processes.

DNA ligases are nucleotidyl transferases that seal breaks in the phosphate-sugar backbone of DNA. DNA ligase play major role in DNA replication, repair and recombination by catalyzing the formation of phosphodiester bonds between adjacent 5′-phosphoryl and 3′-hydroxyl termini at single breaks in double-stranded DNA molecules through an energetically favorable multistep DNA ligation reaction. All DNA ligases utilize the same three-step reaction mechanism: adenylation of DNA ligase, transfer of AMP from Ligase to the 5′-phosphate of nicked DNA, formation of phosphodiester Bond between 3′-OH and 5′-phosphate of Nicked DNA.

In humans, three major types of DNA ligases are reported: DNA ligase I (hligI), DNA ligase III (hligIII) and DNA ligase IV (hligIV). hligI plays an important role in DNA replication by joining Okazaki fragments on the lagging strand of DNA. Apart from this it also plays important roles in DNA damage repair pathways, single strand breaks are repaired by nucleotide excision repair (NER) and base excision repair (BER) pathways. Results of preclinical studies support that Human DNA ligases are attractive target for the development of new anticancer agents for selective inhibition against rapidly proliferating cancer cells.

Human DNA ligase I plays a major role in DNA replication, repair and recombination by catalyzing the formation of phosphodiester bonds between adjacent 5′-phosphoryl and 3′-hydroxyl termini at single breaks in double-stranded DNA molecules through an energetically favorable multistep DNA ligation reaction. Studies have proved that the level of Human DNA Ligase I in human malignant tumor is considerably up-regulated compared with normal tissues and essential for survival of cancer cells. Selective inhibition of Human DNA ligase or selective targeting of DNA repair defects may induce apoptosis in malignant cells.[26]

Singh and Hussain have discoverd a potential novel human DNA ligase I inhibitor 14 from CSIR-CDRI in-house small molecule library by a previously validated pharmacophore based virtual screening method. This compound (S-097/98) demonstrated antiproliferative activities specifically in DLD-1 (colon), MDAMB-231 (triple negative breast) and HepG2 (liver) cancer cell lines at low micromolar concentrations of 6-7 μM. Mechanistic studies show that the compound can directly interacts with the hLigI protein and inhibits ligation *in vitro*, as well as in cell lysate of DLD-1 cells treated with the inhibitor. The compound 14 arrests cell cycle progression at the G2/M phase and increases the nuclear size of DLD-1 cancer cells, thereby demonstrating its antiproliferative activity and finally promotes cellular apoptosis in DLD-1 cells.[27]

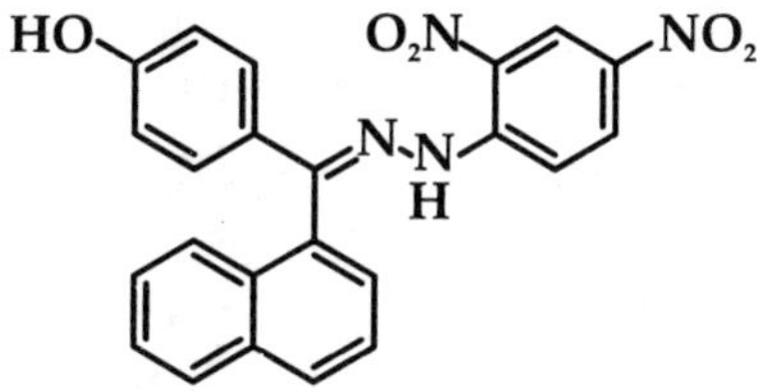

HO, O_2N, NO_2, N, N, H

14

S-097-98

Fig. 15.9: (Z)-4-((2-(2, 4-dinitrophenyl) hydrazono) (naphthalen-1-yl) methyl) phenol; Human DNA ligase I inhibitor (Singh & Hussain 2016)

Inhibitors of HER Signaling Pathway

The human epidermal growth factor receptor 2 (HER2) is a cell membrane tyrosine kinase receptor, member of the epidermal growth factor receptor (EGFR) family, it is over-expressed in approximately 15 - 25% of primary human breast cancers, and is associated with poor clinical outcomes and aggressive tumor progression[28]

Lapatinib (15) is currently approved as first-line therapy in combination with letrozole for patients with MBC who over express HER2 and are estrogen receptor (ER) positive[29, 30], as well as for the treatment of HER2- positive MBC in combination with capecitabine for patients who progressed on prior therapy including a taxane, an anthracycline.[31]

Afatinib (16) is an irreversible small molecule inhibitor, targeting the intracellular tyrosine kinase of the HER-2 molecule. [32] Neratinib (17) is a small molecule irreversible inhibitor against HER1, HER2, and HER4). T AK-285 (18) is a novel inhibitor of HER-2/EGFR tyrosine kinase. ARRY-380 (18) is an orally active, reversible-selective inhibitor of the HER-2 tyrosine kinase receptor with antitumor activity in HER2-positive breast cancer *in vitro* and *in vivo*.

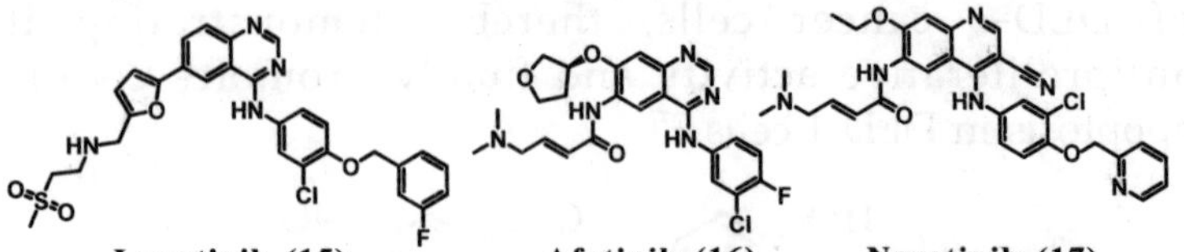

Lapatinib (15) **Afatinib (16)** **Neratinib (17)**

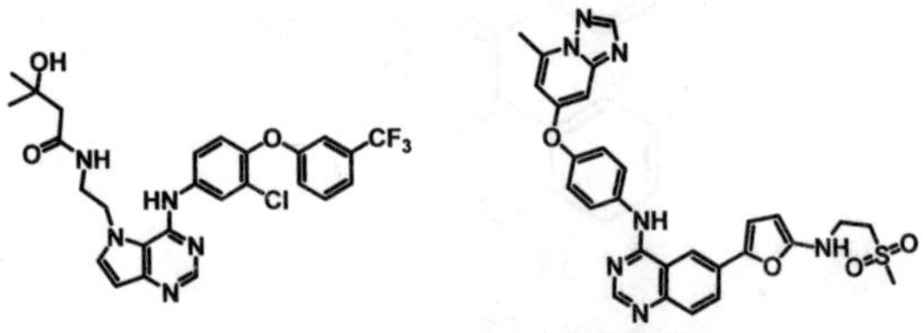

Tak 285 (18) **ARRY-380 (19)**

Fig. 15.10: Structures of some clinically important Anti-HER/EGFR Agents

Inhibitors of PARP1

The poly (adenosine diphosphate [ADP])–ribose) polymerases (PARPs) are a family of enzymes involved in DNA repair, gene transcription, chromatin architecture, and apoptosis in normal human cells.[33] The most abundant is PARP1, a key player in single-stranded DNA base-excision repair. PARP inhibition leads to the accumulation of single strand DNA breaks and subsequent double strand breaks at replication forks that ultimately induce apoptosis and cell death.In normal cells, these breaks are repaired via the homologous recombination double-stranded DNA repair pathway.

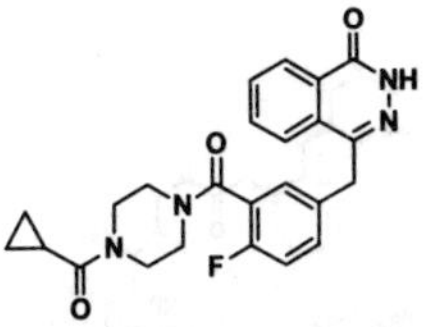

Olaparib/Lynpraza (20)
PARP-1/2/3 IC50 = 4/1/30 nM

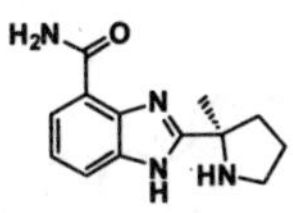

Veliparib (21)
PARP-1/2, Ki = 5.2/2.9 nM

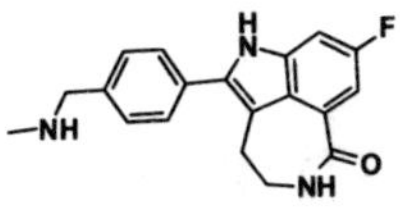

Rucaparib (22)
PARP-1/2, IC50 = 1.4/0.2 nM

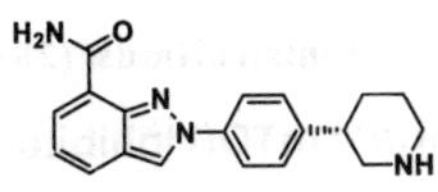

Niraparib (MK4827) (23)
PARP-1/2 IC50 = 3.8/2.1 nM

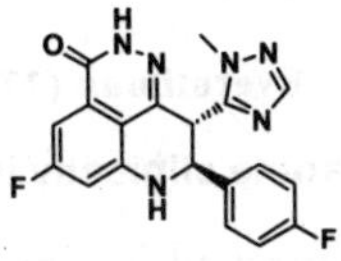

Telazoparib (24)
PARP-1/2 IC50 = 1.2/0.85 nM

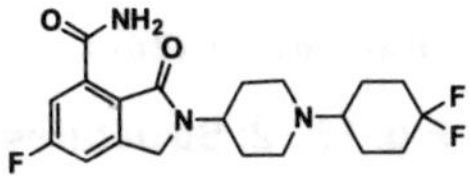

NMS-P118 (25)
PARP 1/2 Kd = 9/1.39 nM

Fig. 15.11: Structures of some clinically important PARPs Inhibitors

The tumor-suppressor proteins BRCA1 and BRCA2 are key components of the DNA repair pathway in humans. The majority of woman with BRCA1 mutations develop triple negative breast cancer.[33] Olaparib (20), Veliparib (21), Rucaparib (22) and Niraparib or MK4827 (23), Telizoparib (24) and NMS-P118 (25) are the most investigated PARP inhibiting agents to date (Fig. 15.11). Olaparib is an orally active PARP-1/2/3 inhibitor that induces apoptosis and cell death in homozygous BRCA-deficient cells.[34] Veliparib is another potent PARP inhibitor, Veliparib is able to potently inhibit both PARP-1 and PARP-2, with K_is (inhibitory constants) of 5.2 and 2.9 nML.[35] Niraparb (MK4827) is a novel potent, orally bioavailable PARP-1 and PARP-2 inhibitor currently in clinical trials for treatment of cancer. It strongly inhibit PARP-1/2 with IC_{50} of 3.8 and 2.1 nM respectively.[36]

Inhibitors of mTOR

The mammalian target of rapamycin (mTOR) is a kinase that is part of the phosphatidylinositol-3-kinase-related kinases (PIKKs) or PI3K-related kinase family.[37] mTOR plays a key role in cell cycle progression, and is inhibited by the antibiotic rapamycin (12).[38] mTOR controls various cellular processes, including growth, survival, and autophagy. Over-activation of PI3K and mTOR has been observed in many cancers.

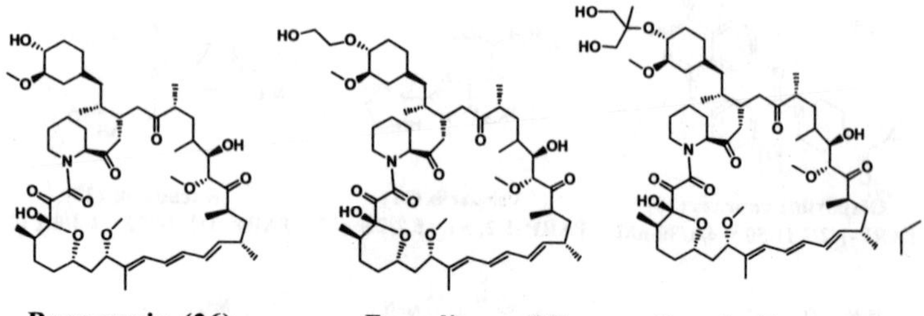

Rapamycin (26) Everolimus (27) Temsirolimus (28)

Fig. 15.12: Structures of some clinically important mTOR Inhibitors

The phosphatidylinositol 3-kinase/mammalian target of rapamycin (PI3K/mTOR) pathway is commonly dysregulated in breast cancer. As such, rapamycin, along with several rapamycin analogues (rapalogs), have been studied for the treatment of a variety of different cancers. Everolimus (13), an mTOR inhibitor, is currently approved for the treatment of hormone receptor (HR)-positive, human epidermal growth factor receptor 2 (HER2)-negative breast cancer.[39] and temsirolimus (14) are currently approved for the treatment of renal cell carcinoma.[40] and mTOR inhibitors have shown promise in a number of other types of cancers, including breast cancer

PI3K Inhibitors

Phosphatidylinositol 3-kinases (PI3K) are a family of enzymes involved in multiple important cellular functions including proliferation, cell growth, differentiation, motility, and survival.[41] Aberrant activation of PI3K has been implicated in different cancers. PI3K promotes estrogen receptor activity, and mutations of PI3K can mediate resistance to endocrine therapy.[42]

Pictilisib (GDC-0941) is the first pan-PI3K inhibitor for which results of randomized trials in ER+ breast cancer have been reported.[43] Clinical trials with PI3K inhibitors in breast cancer patients are still in early phases of development. There have been 2 phase I/II trials reported involving SAR245408 (15) or SAR245409 (16), pan-inhibitors of PI3K.[44]

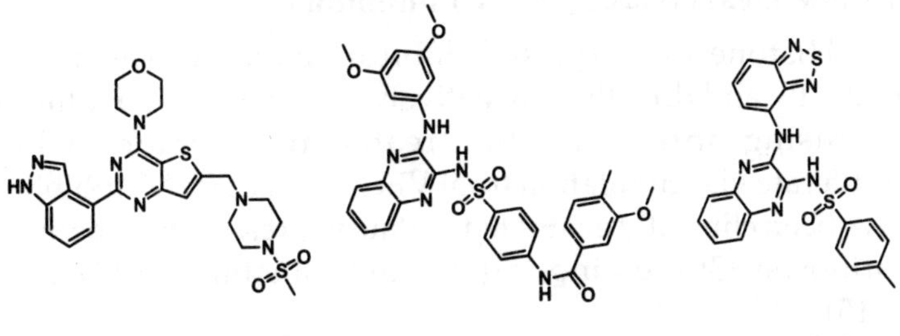

Pictilisib, GDC -0941 (29) SAR245408 (30) SAR245409 (31)

Fig. 15.13: Structures of some clinically important PI3K Inhibitors

Inhibitors of Heat Shock Protein 90 (HSP 90)

HSP 90 is a molecular chaperone protein which assists in the folding and stabilization of proteins vital to cell survival.[45] It assists in the stability and function of many proteins associated with cancer cell propagation, including estrogen receptors, HER2, EGFR, VEGFR, BCR-ABL, AKT, FLT3, MET, BRAF, and CRAF, among others, making it an ideal target for cancer treatment strategies.

Breast cancers that express higher levels of HSP-90 are associated with a higher nuclear grade, larger tumors, increased lymph node involvement, increased expression of HER2 and ER, and more aggressive clinical features. Several different HSP-90 inhibitors including Tanespimycin (32), Retaspimycin (33) and Ganetespib (34) (Fig. 15.14) have recently been studied in phase II trials for HER2 positive population and advanced or MBC.[46]

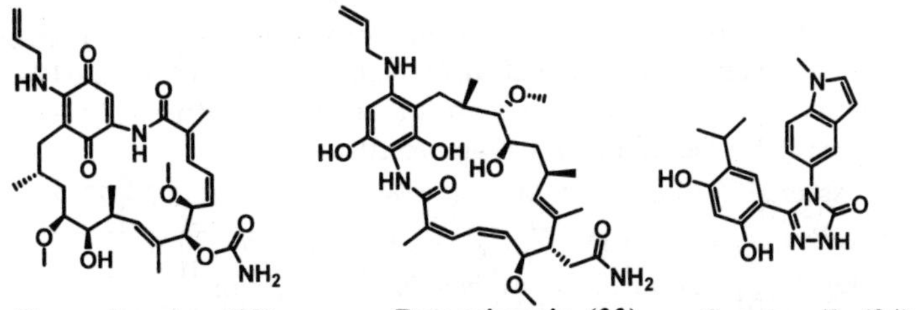

Tenespimycine (32) Retaspimycin (33) Genetespib (34)

Fig. 15.14: Structures of some important PI3K Inhibitors Inhibitors of Heat Shock Protein 90

Histone Deacetylase (HDAC) Inhibitors

Histone deacetylase inhibitors have been shown to indirectly and directly.[51] negatively regulate HIF-1 α, offering promising options for the treatment of tumors, which proliferate via stimulation from VEGF. Three HDAC inhibitors have been clinically evaluated to date in breast cancer patients: vorinostat (35), entinostat(36), and panobinosta (37), Fig. 15.15).[47-48]

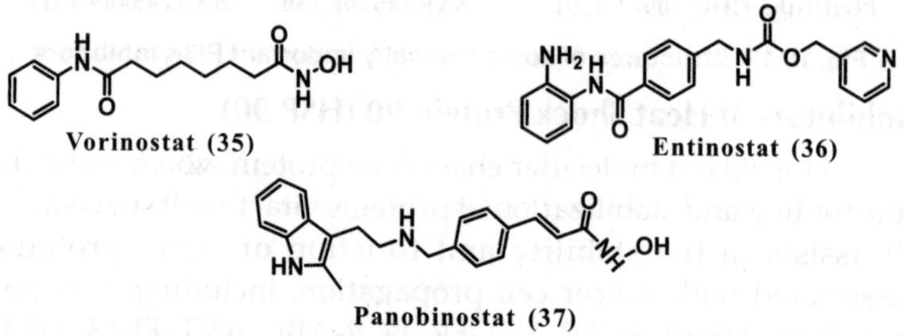

Vorinostat (35)

Entinostat (36)

Panobinostat (37)

Fig. 15.15: Structures of some important HDAC Inhibitors

REFERENCES

1. R.L. Siegel, Kimberly D. Miller and Ahmedin Jemal, *CA Cancer J. Clin.* 2016, 66, 7-30.
2. A. Tfayli, S. Temraz, R. A. Mrad and A. Shamseddine; J Oncol. 2010; 2010: 490631.
3. R.L. Siegel, K.D. Miller, A. Jemal, *CA Cancer J Clin.* 2015, 65, 5-29.
4. M.K. Hussain, M.I. Ansari, N. Yadav, P.K. Gupta, A.K. Gupta, R. Saxena, I. Fatima, M. Manohar, P. Kushwaha, V. Khedgikar, J. Gautam, R. Kant, P.R. Maulik, R. Trivedi, A. Dwivedi, K.R. Kumar, A.K. Saxena, K. Hajela, *RSC Adv.* 2014, 8, 8828-8845.
5. (a) http://www.breastcancerindia.net/statistics/trends.html Retrieved on 16 December 2016. (b) National Cancer Institute USA; https://www.cancer.gov/about-cancer/treatment/drugs/breast#1 Retrieved on 18 December 2016.
6. P. Ascenzi, A. Bocedi, M. Marino, *Mol. Aspects Med.* 2006, *27*, 299.
7. S.T. Pearce, V.C. Jordan, *Crit. Rev. Oncol. Hematol.* 2004, *50*, 3.
8. Ruggiero, R.J., Likis, F.E.*J. Midwif. Women's Health* 2002, *47*, 130.
9. B. McEwen, *Recent Prog. Horm.* 2002, *57*, 357.
10. P. Huang, V. Chandra, F. Rastinejad, *Annu. Rev. Physiol.*, 2010, *72*, 247.

11. C. Thomas, J. Å. Gustafsson, *Nat. Rev. Cancer.*, 2011, *11*, 597.
12. J.A. Katzenellenbogen, *J. Med. Chem.*, 2011, *54*, 5271.
13. S. Nilsson, K.F. Koehler, J. Å. Gustafsson, *Nat. Rev. Drug Discovery.*, 2011, *10*, 778.
14. M.I. Ansari, M.K. Hussain, A. Arun, B. Chakarvarti, R.J Konwar, K. Hajela. E.J. Med. Chem. 2015, 99, 113.
15. R. Saxena, I.Fatima, V.Chandra, C.S. Blesson G. Kharkwal, M.K. Hussain, K. Hajela, B.G. Roy A. Dwivedi, *Steroid*, 2013, 78, 1071.
16. I. Fatima, V. Chandra, R. Saxena, M. Manohar, S. Kitchlu, M.K. Hussain, K.Hajela, and A. Dwivedi, Am J Obstet Gynecol 2011; 205: 362e1-362e11.
17. I.Fatima, R. Saxena, G. Kharkwal, M.K. Hussain, N. Yadav N,K. Hajela *et al. J Steroid Biochem Mol Biol* 2013; 138: 123.
18. V. Chandra I. Fatima, R. Saxena M.K. Hussain, K. Hajela, P. Sankhwar, B.G. Roy, S. Chandna, A. Dwivedi, *Gynecologic Oncology* 2013, 129, 433.
19. V. Chandra, I. Fatima, M. Manohar, P. Popli, M.K. Hussain, K. Hajela, P.L. Sankhwar and A. Dwivedi. *Cell Death & Disease*, 2014, 5, e1380; doi:10.1038/cddis.2014.334.
20. I.M. Ghobrial, T.E. Witzig, A.A. Adjei, *CA Cancer J Clin.* 2005, 55, 178-194.
21. E.A. Slee, C. Adrain, S.J. Martin, J Biol. Chem. 2001, 276, 7320-7326.
22. P.K. Panda, S. Mukhopadhyay, B. Behera, C.S. Bhol, S. Dey, D.N. Das, Life Sci. 2014, 111, 27-35.
23. S.R. Gundala, C. Yang, R. Mukkavilli, R. Paranjpe, M. Brahmbhatt, V. Pannu, *Toxicol Appl. Pharmacol.* 2014, 280, 86-96.
24. J. Wang, J.Z. Li, A. X. Lu, K.F. Zhang, B.J. Li, *Oncol. Lett.* 2014, 7, 1159-1164.
25. D.K. Singh, S. Krishna, S. Chandra, M. Shameem, A.L Deshmukh, and D. Banerjee, *Med. Res. Rev.* 2014, 34: 567.
26. D. Sun, R. Urrabaz, M. Nguyen, J. Marty, S. Stringer, E. Cruz, L. Medina-Gundrum, S. Weitman, *Clin. Cancer Res.*, 2001, *7*, 4143-4148; (b). D.E. Barnes, A.E. Tomkinson, A.R. Lehmann, A.D.B. Webster, and T. Lindahl, *Cell*, 1992, *69*, 495.
27. D. K. Singh, M.K. Hussain, S. Krishna, A.L. Deshmukh, M. Shameem, P. Maurya, K. Hajela, M.I. Siddiqi and D. Banerjee, *RSC Adv.*, 2016, 6, 94574.
28. G.E. Konecny, M.D. Pegram, N. Venkatesan, R. Finn, G. Yang, M. Rahmeh, M. Untch, D.W. Rusnak, G. Spehar, R.J. Mullin, B.R. Keith, T.M. Gilmer, M. Berger, K.C. Podratz, D.J. Slamon, *Cancer Res*, 2006, *66*, 630.

29. H.L. Gomez, G. Romieu, A. Manikhas, M.J. Kennedy, M.F. Press, J Maltzman, A. Florance, L. O'Rourke, C. Oliva, S. Stein, M. Pegram. *J Clin Oncol*, 2009, *27*, 5538.
30. G.D.L. Lewis, G.Li, D.L. Dugger, L.M. Crocker, K.L. Parsons, E.Mai, W.A. Blattler, J.M. Lambert, R.V. Chari, R.J. Lutz, W.L. Wong, F.S. Jacobson H. Koeppen, R.H. Schwall, S. R.K. Mitra, S.D. Spencer, *Cancer Res.*, 2008, *68*, 9280.
31. (a). T.A. Yap, L. Vidal, J. Adam, *et al. J, Clin, Oncol.*, 2010, 28, 3965; (b). T. Hickish, D. Wheatley, N. Lin, *et al., J, Clin, Oncol.*, 2009, 27(15S): Abstract 1023.
32. (c). K. Gunzer *et al. Cancer Res.*, 2009, *69* (24 Suppl): Abstract 4098; (b). M.H. Schuler, *et al., J, Clin, Oncol*, 2010, *28*: abstr 1065; (c). N. Harbeck, M. Schmidt, P. Harter *et al. Cancer Res.*, 2009, 69(24 Suppl): Abstract 5062.
33. (a). H.J. Burstein, *Semin Oncol*, 2011, *38* (Suppl 2): S17-S24; (b). H. Farmer, N. McCabe, C. J. Lord, *et al.* Nature, 2005, *434*, 917; (c). L.A. Carey *et al. N, Engl, J, Med.*, 2011, *364*, 277. (c) A. Tutt, M. Robson, J. E. Garber, *et al. breast cancer: A proof-of Concept Trial. Lancet.*, 2010, *376*, 235.
34. S.X. Yang, S. Kummar, S.M. Steinberg, A.J. Murgo, M. Gutierrez *et al. Cancer Biol Ther*, 2009, *8*, 2004.
35. L.M. Wagner, Onco Targets Ther. 2015; 8: 1931-1939.
36. N.S. Gavande, P.S. V.Vere-Carozza, H.D. Hinshaw, S.I. Jalal, C.R. Sears, K.S. Pawelczak[c], Jn J. Turchi, *Pharmacology & Therapeutics*, 2016, 160, 65-83.
37. C. Vézina,A. Kudelski, S.N. Sehgal, *J, Antibiot*, (Tokyo). 1975, *28*, 721.
38. (a). G.G. Chiang, R.T. Abraham. *Trends Mol Med.*, 2007, *13*, 433; (b). G. Hudes, M. Carducci, *et al. N Engl J Med.*, 2007, *356*, 2271; (c). R. J. Motzer, B. Escudier, S. Oudard, *et al. Lancet.*, 2008, *372*, 449-56.
39. J. JX Lee, K. Loh, and Y-S. Yap, Cancer Biol Med. 2015, 12, 342-354.
40. G.E. Stoica, T.F. Franke, M. Moroni, *et al. Oncogene*, 2003, *22*, 7998.
41. (a). S. Tolaney, *et al. Cancer Res*, 2011, 71, 240; (b). J. Baselga, S. Tolaney, L. Hart, P. Gomez, E. Gartner, A. DeCillis, R. Ruiz-Soto, J. Lager, H.Burris *Cancer Res*, 2011, 243.
42. P. Schoffski, E. De Benedictis, S. Gendreau, L. Gianni, I. E. Krop G. Levy *Cancer Res*, 2011, *150*.
43. C.X. Ma, *The American Journal of Hematology/Oncology*, 2015, 11, 23.
44. I. Brana and L.L. Siu, BMC Medicine 2012, 10: 161.

45. U. Banerji. *Clin Cancer Res.*, 2009, *15*, 9.
46. K. Jhaveri, S. Ochiana, M. PS Dunphy *et al.* Expert Opin Investig Drugs. 2014 May; 23(5): 611-628.
47. P. Schoffski, E. De Benedictis, S. Gendreau, L. Gianni, I.E. Krop G. Levy *Cancer Res*, 2011, *150*.
48. X. Kong, Z. Lin, D. Liang, D. Fath, N. Sang, *J. Mol Cell Biol.*, 2006 *26*, 2019; (b). S. H. Kim, K.W. Kim, J.W. Jeong, *et al. Oncol Rep.*, 2007, 17, 793.

Pages: 164-168

Renewable Resources and Environment
Edited by: Dr. Baby Tabassum
ISBN: 978-93-5056-893-4
Edition: 2018
Published by: Discovery Publishing House Pvt. Ltd., New Delhi (India)

A Review on Zinc Telluride Sintered Films

Seema Teotia

ABSTRACT

II-VI semiconductor Zinc telluride is a binary chemical compound with the formula ZnTe. This solid material with a direct band gap of 2.26 eV is usually a p-type semiconductor. Its crystal structure is cubic, like that for sphalerite and diamond but can be also prepared as hexagonal crystals (wurtzite structure). Zinc telluride can be easily doped, and for this reason it is one of the more common semiconducting materials used in optoelectronics. ZnTe is important for development of various semiconductor devices, including blue LEDs, laser diodes, solar cells, and components of microwave generators. The material can also be used as a component of ternary semiconductor compounds, such as $Cd_xZn_{(1-x)}Te$ (conceptually a mixture composed from the end-members ZnTe and CdTe), which can be made with a varying composition x to allow the optical band gap to be tuned as desired. In the present paper we will report some review work on ZnTe sintered films.

Keywords: *Band gap, Hexagonal, Semiconductor, Sphalerite, Wurtzite.*

Department of Physics, Govt. Raza P.G. College, Rampur - 244 901 (U.P.) (India)
email: Seemateotia73@gmail.com

INTRODUCTION

Zinc telluride (ZnTe) thin films are widely used in modern technologies of solid-state devices (light-emitting diodes, solar cells, photo detectors, etc.) because of its excellent characteristics, namely large energy band gap, low resistivity, high transparency in visible spectral domain,[1-4] etc. For this compound, there is a very sensitive and complex dependence of film micro structure on preparation method and deposition conditions[5-8]. In this connection, many studies have recently been reported to establish the deposition conditions in order to obtain ZnTe films having a particular crystalline structure, desired optical properties and also the morphology[2-6, 9].

A variety of preparation techniques have been reported so far to obtain device-grade ZnTe thin films. Some of them are: thermal evaporation[5], vapour phase epitaxy[6], molecular beam epitaxy[7], hot wall epitaxy[10], metal organic vapour phase epitaxy[11], r.f. sputtering[12], electro synthesis[13], stacked elemental layer (SEL)[14] etc.

The sintered films have advantages like; ease of processing, cost effectiveness and no sophisticated technology is required for device fabrication. Although many devices have been developed to date from sintered materials but the search is still on for newer configuration and compositions and bring down the physical size of the device to the micro miniature level in the form of sintered films..The sintered films offer two main advantages, flexibility in fabrication of films of good quality, which makes them suitable for optoelectronic devices, and that their optical energy band gap can be varied through processing. These devices have recently become the focus of intensive fundamental and applied studies. The main advantages of sintered films are: low cost technology reducing conventional thin film deposition method, case of modification and adjustment of optical properties like energy band gap and absorption characteristics, a varied substrate choice, relatively low temperature processing and possibility of coating on hybrid circuits, interfacing with electrical or optical device[15, 16].

PREPARATION OF ZnTe SAMPLE

To prepare sintered ZnTe films, a calculated amount of ZnTe powder, 10% of ZnTe, $ZnCl_2$ and few drops of ethylene glycol were thoroughly mixed. The paste thus prepared was screen printed on ultra clean glass substrate to get the film of ZnTe. The sample thus prepared was dried at 120° C for 4 hour in nitrogen atmosphere in a tube furnace. The reason for drying the sample at lower temperature was to avoid cracks in the sample. The melting point of zinc chloride, which is used as an adhesive, is 283° C however the evaporation of cadmium chloride starts at lower temperature. Zinc chloride is hygroscopic so to get a stable sintered film, zinc chloride and organic material should not remain in the sample, So after drying, the sample was sintered at 500° C for 10 min in tube furnace, to remove the organic materials left which have been used as a binder in the formation of paste. For drying and sintering nitrogen atmosphere is used instead of open atmosphere because in open atmosphere ZnTe reacts with atmospheric oxygen and the formation of zinc oxide (ZnO) occurs. But in nitrogen atmosphere this problem does not exist.

RESULT AND DISCUSSION

S. Sirohi *et al* studied the optical and structural properties of ZnTe sintered films and reported band gap measurement from reflection spectra by using Tauc relation[17] and X ray diffraction pattern[18].

S. Teotia *et al* studied the variation of band gap of ZnTe films with sintering temperature and reported that band gap increases with increase in sintering temperature because average grain size and crystallinity increases with increase in temperature[19].

S. Teotia *et al* studied the electrical properties of ZnTe sintered films and reported a plot of Ln J_F versus V_F and current voltage characteristic which shows good diode characteristics. S. Teotia *et al* also reported the barrier height of ZnTe film which comes out to be 0.508 eV[20].

V. Kumar *et al* studied the reflection spectra by UV reflection spectroscopy and calculate the band gaps Eg of the films and reported the hexagonal (wurtzite) structure of the films confirmed by x-ray diffraction analysis and the surface morphology of films by the scanning electron microscopy technique. V. Kumar *et al* also reported the DC conductivity of the films measured in vacuum using a two-probe technique and reported that this investigation will be useful in characterizing ZnTe for its applications in photovoltaics[21].

S.Sirohi *et al* studied the band gap measurement of sintered ZnTe films from reflection and absorption spectra and concluded that the reflection technique to calculate the band gap energy is more accurate and faster method than any other method in case of sintered films[22].

REFERENCES

1. Jain, M. (Ed), II-VI Semiconductor Compounds, World Scientific, 1993.
2. Bhargava, R. (Ed), Properties of Wide Band gap II-VI Semiconductors. Inspec, 1997.
3. Rohatgi, A., Ringel, S.A., Sudharsanan, R., Meyers, P.V., Liu, C.H., Ramanathan, V. Investigation of CdZnTe, CdMnTe, and CdTe Polycrystalline Films for Photovoltaic Applications Solar Cells 27 1989: pp. 219-230.
4. Kalita, P.K., Sarma, B.K., Das, H.L. Photo Response Characteristics of Vacuum Evaporated ZnTe Thin Films, Indian Journal of Pure and Applied Physics 37 1999: pp. 885-890.
5. Aqili, A.K.S., Ali, Z., Mazsood, A. Optical and Structural Properties of Two-sourced Evaporated ZnTe Thin Films Applied Surface Science 167 2000: pp. 1-11. http://dx.doi.org/10.1016/S0169-4332(00)00498-0111
6. Khan, M.R.H. Interface Properties of a CdTe-ZnTe Hetero Junction Journal Physics D: Applied Physics 271994: pp. 2190-2193. http://dx.doi.org/10.1088/0022-3727/27/10/031.
7. Tao, W.I., Jurkovic, M., Wang, I.N. Doping of ZnTe by Molecular Beam Epitaxy Applied Physics Letter 641994: pp. 1848-1849.
8. Rusu, G. I., Prepelita, P., Apetroaei, N., Popa, G. On the Electronic Transport and Optical Properties of ZnTe Thin Films Journal of Optoelectronics and Advanced Material 7 (2) 2005: pp. 829-835.

9. Mahalingam, T., John, V.S., Rajendran, S., Ravi, G., Sebastian, P.J. Annealing Studies of Electro deposited ZincTelluride Thin Films Surface Coatings Technology 1552002: pp. 245-249.
10. Merchant, J.D., Cocivera, M. Properties of Zinc Telluride Containing Impurities Introduced during Spray Pyrolysis, Journal of Electrochemistry Society 143 1996: pp. 4054-4059.
11. Wolf, K., Stanz, H., Naumov, A., Wagner, H.P., Kuhn,W., Hahn, B., Gebhardt, W. Growth and Doping of ZnTe and ZnSe Epilayers with Metal Organic Vapour Phase Epitaxy Journal of Crystal Growth 138 1994: pp. 412-417.
12. Tokumitsu, Y., Kawabuchi, A., Kitayama, H., Imura, T., Osaka, Y., Nishiyama, F. Evaluation of Epitaxial ZnTe Films Prepared by RF Sputtering by Means of Ion Beam Channeling, Japan Journal Applied Physics 29 1990: pp. 1039-1042.
13. Konigtein, C., Neumann-Spallart, M. Mechanistic Studies on the Electro Deposition of ZnTe, Journal of Electrochemical Society 145 1998: pp. 337-343. http://dx.doi.org/10.1149/1.1838256
14. Subramani S., Devarajan M., Optical Properties and Surface Morphology of Zinc Telluride Thin Films Prepared by Stacked Elemental Layer Method, Materials Science (Med•iagotyra). 18, 2. 2012, pp. 107-111.
15. Teotia S., Sharma T.P., Mishra S.C.K., SPIE, 1999, Vol. 3903, pp. 298-304.
16. Teotia S., "Sintered Semiconducting Films: A Review" J. of Scientific and Applied Research, 6(1) (January 2015) ISSN: 0975-9743, pp. 21-22.
17. Tauc, J., Ed., Amorphous and Liquid Semiconductors, Plenum, New York, 1974, p. 159.
18. Sirohi S., Kumar V., Kumar V., Sharma T.P., Semiconductor Materials, R.K. Bedi (Ed.) 1998, pp. 91-94.
19. Teotia S., Sharma T.P., Proceedings ISOAP-2006 p. 5.
20. Teotia S., Sharma T.P., Proceedings ISOAP-2006 p. 8.
21. Kumar V., Kumar V., Dwivedi, D.K., Physica Scripta, 2012, 86 (1) 015604.
22. Sirohi S., Sharma V.K., Sharma T.P., C.S.I.O. 6(2), (1998), pp. 95-99.

Index